SUBVERSIVE WOMEN

THOEMMES

In appreciation of David Lytton Cobbold, Rosina Bulwer Lytton's great-great-grandson, and his wife, Christine, for their support and encouragement of the Rosina revival and for placing a tombstone on her unmarked grave.

A BLIGHTED LIFE

Rosina Bulwer Lytton

With a new Introduction by
Marie Mulvey Roberts

THOEMMES PRESS

© Thoemmes Press 1994

Published in 1994 by

Thoemmes Press
85 Park Street
Bristol BS1 5PJ
England

ISBN 1 85506 248 8

This is a reprint of the 1880 Edition

Publisher's Note

These reprints are taken from original copies of each book. In many cases the condition of those originals is not perfect, the paper, often handmade, having suffered over time and the copy from such things as inconsistent printing pressures resulting in faint text, show-through from one side of a leaf to the other, the filling in of some characters, and the break up of type. The publisher has gone to great lengths to ensure the quality of these reprints but points out that certain characteristics of the original copies will, of necessity, be apparent in reprints thereof.

Not the green graves where loved ones sleep,
　And friends strew grief with flowers,
Where circling years their vigils keep,
　'Mid snows and summer hours…

No, – 'tis those dark undaisied graves,
　Dug deep within the heart,
Where memory like a maniac raves
　O'er wrongs that *can't* depart.

Rosina Bulwer Lytton

Lady Bulwer Lytton

IN A

LUNATIC ASYLUM.

THE

SOMERSET County Gazette

Of to-morrow, the 10th instant,

WILL CONTAIN

A FULL ACCOUNT

Of the proceedings in this extraordinary case.

INTRODUCTION

Rosina Bulwer Lytton has been dismissed generally as the mad wife of the novelist and politician, Edward Bulwer-Lytton, and her literary productions and extraordinary single-handed campaign for the rights of women have been largely forgotten.

In most of her 14 novels, the collection of essays and the volumes of letters, that were written between 1839 and 1871, she draws attention to the inequalities existing between the sexes, particularly the powerlessness of married women under the law. Her own plight is expressed in a controversial memoir, *A Blighted Life: A True Story* (1880), in which she accuses her husband of abuse, neglect and cruelty. The title of this polemic epitomizes how Rosina Bulwer Lytton regarded her own situation as a woman living in Victorian England. Her account may be interpreted in a number of different ways: as a personal vendetta intended to destroy the reputation of an eminent man for example, or as the case-history of a female hysteric who had been committed by her husband to a lunatic asylum. A feminist interpretation would see the text as representing a narrative of resistance, as articulating a discourse of disobedience and subversion of the feminine role. Whatever the reader's verdict may be, whether to vilify or vindicate its autobiographical subject, it cannot be denied that the author was a woman of great vitality, wit and intelligence who experienced intense suffering through the loss of her children and, for a time, her liberty.

In the autobiography that she had been preparing shortly before her death, Rosina Bulwer Lytton laments that 'The first mistake I made was being born at all'.[1] The most immediate explanation for this cynical statement was the fact that her father, Francis Massey Wheeler, had wanted a boy. When Rosina was born on a 'dreary, drizzling November morning'[2] in 1802, the nurse was too afraid to break the bad news to him. It was left to the infant's mother's sister, Bessie Doyle, to tell him the 'disagreeable tidings'.[3] That she had registered that the birth of Rosina was not a joyful event is evident from Rosina's aunt's response to the father's reaction: 'Well, we can't strangle the poor little thing; since it has pleased God to send it, it must live.'[4] From this inauspicious beginning, Rosina grew up to be a troublesome and rebellious child in a dilapidated castle at Ballywire, Lizzard Connell, near Limerick, on the West coast of Ireland. In this latter-day Castle Rackrent,[5] domestic discord and a belief in the supernatural prevailed. There is mention of a banshee whose nocturnal wail was believed by the local population to be a harbinger

---

[1] Louisa Devey, *Life of Rosina, Lady Lytton* (London: Sonnenschein, 1887), p. 1. In her published work, Rosina does not use a hyphen in her surname Bulwer Lytton unlike her husband.

[2] *Loc, cit.*

[3] *ibid.*, p. 2.

[4] *Loc. cit.*

[5] Rosina Bulwer Lytton was familiar with the work of Maria Edgeworth, whose novel, *Castle Rackrent* (1800) is about an Anglo-Irish family headed by the drunken Sir Patrick, who bears some resemblance to Francis Wheeler.

of doom.[6] For Rosina Bulwer Lytton, this would prove to be prophetic. The children's nurse, Nelly, was also superstitious and told Rosina and her sister, Henrietta, when they were naughty that they would be abducted by sirens and mermaids. As it turned out, the children, along with their aunt, were removed from the family home and taken on a dangerous stormy sea voyage, not by supernatural beings or demi-gods but by their mother, Anna Wheeler, who was soon to be deified as the 'Goddess of Reason'.

Not since Mary Wollstonecraft and Mary Shelley and before Emmeline and Christabel Pankhurst has there been such an important mother and daughter relationship in terms of feminism and radicalism, scandal and controversy, polemic and literary productivity as that of Anna Wheeler and Rosina Bulwer Lytton. Both campaigned tirelessly for the cause of women in their writings and throughout their lives, actively and audibly protesting against the restrictions imposed upon them as daughters, wives and mothers. Arguably the most influential feminist writer between Mary Wollstonecraft and Emmeline Pankhurst, Anna Wheeler was the co-author with William Thompson of *Appeal of One Half the Human Race, Women, Against the Pretensions of the Other Half, Men, to Retain Them in Political, and Thence in Civil and Domestic, Slavery* (1825).[7]

---

[6] A banshee is mentioned at the beginning of Rosina Bulwer Lytton's autobiographical novel, *Miriam Sedley*, 3 vols (London: Newby, 1850), pp. 2–3.

[7] William Thompson and Anna Wheeler, *Appeal of One Half the Human Race, Women, Against the Pretensions of the Other Half, Men, to Retain Them in Political, and Thence in Civil and Domestic, Slavery; in Reply to a Paragraph of Mr. Mill's Celebrated 'Article on Government'* (London: Longman, 1825), also republished in this series as volume II, *Subversive Women* (Bristol: Thoemmes, 1994).

Her protest against the way in which women were reduced to involuntary breeding machines and household slaves, subject to men's pernicious despotism is likely to have been informed, at least in part, by her own disastrous marriage. The daughter of Archdeacon Doyle and godchild of Henry Gratton, she rashly married Francis Wheeler, at the age of sixteen,[8] as a reason for escaping her family home. The ploy turned out to have been ill-conceived, as her young husband was a drunken, dissipated, fox-hunting wastrel, who appeared to care more for his horse, Dare-Devil, than for his new family. According to Anna Wheeler, as far as a husband is concerned his wife 'has not become his servant – for servants, if ill-used, may depart and try to better themselves elsewhere – but his serf, his slave, whom, according to Judge Butler, (himself a married man), he may correct with a stick of the thickness of his thumb'.[9]

Managing to break with her own serfdom, Anna Wheeler departed for Guernsey with her sister, Bessie, and two daughters to live with their uncle, John Doyle, who was the Governor of the island. From there, they travelled to France, where Anna Wheeler absorbed the ideas of Saint-Simonian feminism. The feminist militancy that she eventually brought with her to London was to prove to be too radical for her Liberal associates. As a result she would transfer her allegiances to Owenite Socialist circles and in 1833 would begin writing articles for Robert Owen's paper, *The Crisis*.

---

[8] There was a suggestion that she was 15 but Devey inclines towards the opinion that she was 16. *Life of Rosina*, p. 5.

[9] Anon., [Anna Wheeler], *The Crisis* (August 31, 1833), p. 278.

Her training as a radical had started while she was in Ireland, partly as a means of militating against her unfortunate marriage. While her sister read Minerva Press novels and shed tears over the 'delicate distresses'[10] of their sentimental heroines, Anna Wheeler immersed herself in the political philosophies of the radical thinkers of the French Revolution and especially the writings of Mary Wollstonecraft.

The children were exposed to both influences, the cult of sensibility favoured by one and the feminist radicalism extolled by the other. But the ideology that Rosina was to inherit was that of her mother. Although they became kindred spirits in later life, during the early years the relationship between mother and daughter was far from idyllic, as Louisa Devey points out in her *Life of Rosina, Lady Lytton* (1887).

The most revealing account is given in Rosina Bulwer Lytton's fictional autobiography, *Miriam Sedley* (1850), in which Anna Wheeler is portrayed as the heroine's Aunt Marley. True to real life, the fictionalized character, though an advocate of Enlightenment ideas of tolerance and rationality, was far from reasonable in practice, particularly as regards child-care. A revealing episode tells of how Rosina's fictional counterpart, Miriam, was entertaining Lady L. in the nursery, when Aunt Marley swept into the room and boxed her niece's ears. So violent was this outburst that she smashed Lady L.'s head-gear and barley-water ornaments, and, we are told, all but broke Miriam's nose into the bargain. The cause of all this, the author attributes ironically to 'my Aunt's gentle reproofs, which were no doubt part of the

[10] Devey, *Life of Rosina*, p. 8.

system of universal benevolence and general philanthropy'.[11]

Anna Wheeler took every opportunity to proselytize, even in circumstances that were not condusive to her oratory like the sea voyage to Guernsey. Her insistence that the captain run his ship according to democratic principles was undeterred by his opposition and the ferocious storm that was blowing. As it turned out, both her arguments and the vessel ran aground and so the passengers were forced to make for Milford Haven in an open boat. On the eventual arrival at the Governor's House in Guernsey, they embarked upon a new and more affluent way of life. Michael Sadleir mischievously suggests that Anna Wheeler enjoyed a temporary lapse from egalitarianism for a semi-regal existence over the next four years. This was made possible by John Doyle's extravagant life-style which resulted in him accumulating over £20,000 of debts. Eventually he was forced to abandon his creditors along with the people of Guernsey, and depart with Anna Wheeler, her sister and daughters to London.

Rosina and Henrietta were enrolled at a school in Kensington which is fictionalized as Miss James's school for young ladies in *Miriam Sedley*. It is described there as being 'about as interesting and instructive to us as the being condemned to three or four pages of ragged school A.B.C. work would have been to Locke, or to Isaac Newton'.[12] The paucity of educational opportunities available for girls was compounded by the fact, as the heroine observed, that if a woman dared to unfold her intellectual wings for the same educational journey as men then she risked

[11] Bulwer Lytton, *Miriam Sedley*, II, p. 271.

[12] *ibid.*, p. 278.

being seen as an aberration of the female sex. Comparing her to a bat, she claims that such a woman was 'not tolerated by the hawks of men, and pulled to pieces by the cats of women'.[13] The scarcity within her own class of any female solidarity against male hegemony, had always been a source of frustration for Rosina Bulwer Lytton. Unlike her mother who had experienced more closely the impact of the female radicals of the 1790s, she was suffering the back-lash against the French Revolution and other radical elements that had emerged from the Rational Enlightenment. In a society that privileged masculinity and foregrounded the achievements of men, it is hardly surprising to find her comparing the effect of a man entering an all-female company with that of switching on a light-bulb in a dark room. The flutter of female affectation vying for his attention to light up their lives, contrasts with the dullness and apathy which had preceded his arrival.[14] Glimmers of resistance to such scenarios emerged from the burgeoning feminism of the mid-nineteenth century that developed into the New Woman movement which met fierce resistance during the fin-de-siécle. However in her preface to *Very Successful* (1856), Rosina Bulwer Lytton refers satirically to negative representations of the New Woman as a member of a tribe of masculine women who were 'nature's worst anomalies' because they sought independence, education and personal freedom. Often caricatured as struggling with a bicycle and bloomers, the New Woman stood in stark opposition to the Angel in the House, who epitomized the purity and submission of

[13] *Loc. cit.*

[14] *ibid.*, I, p. 230.

Victorian womanhood, and to the cult of the invalid, which emphasized the delicacy, refinement and susceptibility to illness of the well-bred lady.[15]

The way in which the ideals of femininity were exaggerated is perhaps best illustrated in Rosina Bulwer Lytton's work by Miss Seraphina in the novel *Cheveley or, The Man of Honour* (1839) who prepares herself to make an elegant and timely swoon into the arms of a man. The socially constructed role of female passivity was rejected by the young Rosina Doyle Wheeler who grew up from a tomboy into a woman who regarded herself to be the equal of any man. In her refusal to subscribe to the assumption that the female intellect was inferior to that of men she rejected the commonly-held belief that the Victorian woman had a 'head almost too small for intellect but just big enough for love'.[16] By the middle of the nineteenth century, women were discouraged from educating or improving their minds in the belief that their brains differed physiologically from those of men's. According to contemporary theories of sexual difference, male cells were believed to be *katabolic* or active while female brain cells were thought to be *anabolic* or passive and subject to a fixed energy expenditure. What was inferred from this was that women could not spare for intellectual development too many brain cells, as these were normally reserved for reproductive purposes.[17] It proved to be Rosina

[15] See chapter II 'The Cult of Invalidism' in Bram Dijkstra, *Idols of Perversity: Fantasies of Feminine Evil in Fin-De-Siécle Culture* (London: Oxford University Press, 1986), pp. 25–63.

[16] Quoted by Jane Usher, *Women's Madness: Misogyny or Mental Illness?* (London: Harvester/Wheatsheaf, 1991), p. 68.

[17] See Elaine Showalter, *The Female Malady: Women, Madness and English Culture, 1830–1980* (London: Virago, 1987), p. 122 who explains that this was the theory propounded by Patrick Geddes and J. Arthur Thompson in *The Evolution of Sex* (1889).

Bulwer Lytton's misfortune that she had left so much room in her mind for love since this was to lead to the disasters that were to blight her life.

Romance blossomed when the dazzling beauty that she had inherited from her mother attracted the attentions of Edward Bulwer-Lytton. The courtship was mediated by Lady Caroline Lamb, whose insights were assisted by the fact of her having been romantically involved not only with Byron but even more appropriately, with Edward Bulwer-Lytton himself. The parallels between the two women did not end there. Both rebelled against the prescribed roles of femininity to such an extent that their relatives tried to certify them insane. Writing fiction provided them with a means of therapy and empowerment in the aftermath of unhappy love affairs. Caroline Lamb's novel *Glenarvon* (1816) concerning her relationship with Byron is the equivalent of Rosina Bulwer Lytton's *Cheveley*, which is about Edward Bulwer-Lytton.[18]

Within her novels, Rosina Bulwer Lytton explores the tyranny of romantic love and the way in which it lures women into the unequal partnership of marriage. These were views which she shared with her mother whose mouthpiece, Aunt Marley in *Miriam Sedley*, tries to persuade Miriam not to marry young Sedley by insisting:

> Marriage was a great social error, a Boeotian mistake, – (if so, it is the very worst of all mistakes, as there is no remedy for it) – but as, in the present barbarous state of civilization, husbands were the necessary consequence of this fatal error, young

---

[18] Edward Bulwer-Lytton inscribed in his copy of *Glenarvon*, a handsome tribute to Caroline Lamb.

Sedley would do as well for a tyrant as any other fool.[19]

Towards the end of the novel, Miriam, as the true daughter of the Goddess of Reason, interrupts her suitor's courtship with expositions on the hazards of romantic love and marriage. But, however mindful she was of these dangers, she disregarded them to the extent of contemplating marriage, as did her real-life, counterpart, Rosina Bulwer Lytton.

That the match was destined for disaster was immediately apparent to Elizabeth Bulwer-Lytton, Edward's mother, who tried to prevent it at all costs. She did succeed in delaying the wedding by accusing her future daughter-in-law of being two years older than she had claimed. But after this allegation was proved false, the ceremony went ahead on 29 August 1827. The reaction of the groom's mother was to withdraw not only herself, but also her large fortune from the newly-weds. As a consequence of this maternal deprivation, Edward Bulwer-Lytton was obliged to earn a living through novel-writing. The strains arising from shortage of money, the birth of two children, Robert and Emily, and Rosina Bulwer Lytton's refusal to conform to the expected role of wife led to marital conflicts that were sometimes violent. Sensationalist stories of the tempestuous marriage circulated among their contemporaries. One incident involved Edward Bulwer-Lytton threatening his wife with a knife and then biting a chunk out of her cheek. Another occasion was made literally more heated when Rosina Bulwer Lytton consigned her husband's favourite shirt to the flames. Attacks and

[19] Bulwer Lytton, *Miriam Sedley*, II, p. 14.

counter-attacks were to continue throughout their lives. For example, Rosina Bulwer Lytton flirted with a prince in Naples in retaliation for Edward Bulwer-Lytton's numerous infidelities while he was busy writing *The Last Days of Pompeii* (1834). But because of the double standard that prevailed, it was as a result of *her* action that their days of married life were numbered.

In 1836, after nearly nine years of marriage, the couple drew up an agreement to separate. The laws affecting women, whether married or separated, put them at a distinct political and economic disadvantage. Although Rosina Bulwer Lytton wryly noted that England is the best country 'for men and horses', she concludes that it is 'the very worst in the whole universe for those peculiar beasts of burden, called wives'.[20] Prior to the Marriage and Divorce Act of 1857 and the Woman's Property Act passed in 1882, women were not allowed to divorce their spouses, sue for alimony, lay claim to their earnings, property or possessions, however personal, or even to the custody of their children. According to Louisa Devey, Edward Bulwer-Lytton exercised his right to remove his son and daughter from their mother. For her this was a terrible deprivation. Apart from four months in 1858, she never saw Robert again from the age of 7 and was even denied access to Emily ten years earlier, while she lay dying of typhus fever. Resentment of her powerlessness in law, as a wife and mother, echoes throughout her fiction. The root cause was the institution of marriage, for, as she argues in her novel, *A School for Husbands* (1852):

---

[20] Rosina Bulwer Lytton, *Memoirs of a Muscovite*, 3 vols (London: Newby, London, 1844), I, p. 161.

> By convention, marriage annihilates a woman's
> power and renders her a nullity; this disenfran-
> chizement from all individual privilege and
> independence has not, and cannot have, a moral
> tendency, for it is unjust; since then, her sphere is
> placed within the orbit of her husband.[21]

Because wives were refused protection from the law,
women were left vulnerable to the will of a possibly
tyrannical husband. In view of this, Rosina Bulwer
Lytton urges women to vet future partners carefully,
since:

> every law respecting marriage, as it now exists, is
> wrong, rotten, and monstrous, [and] every woman
> of principle, before she submits to be branded for
> life at the matrimonial galleys, and her chain locked
> on, should look well to the character of the man
> with whom she is to be coupled.[22]

The analogy with slavery is significant because, like
slaves who take on the names of their masters,
women, when they marry lose their family name and
are given that of their husband. The politics of
naming was indicative of how in practice wives did
not exist in the eyes of the law. Rosina Bulwer Lytton
referred to herself as branded by the name of her
husband. She highlights the inequalities between men
and women in relation to marriage by reversing the
husband and wife role in *Behind the Scenes* (1854).
In a satire on husbands, she declares that the ideal
husband is almost a myth:

---

[21] Rosina Bulwer Lytton, *A School for Husbands: or Moliére's Life and
Times*, 3 vols (London: Skeet, 1852), III, p. 114.

[22] *ibid.*, I, p. 312.

that is, he was seldom heard of, and *never* seen. In
fact, the poor man was always ill, which is a way
some men have, of giving their wives their
widowhood by instalments, and like money paid in
the same way, though it is not so advantageous as
the sum total, still, in both instances, it evinces an
effort to do what is right...a more innocuous,
self-sufficing, tractable, liberal, non-exacting,
never-grumbling, anti-Lord-and-masterish, animal
of the genus husband, never existed; for live he did
not, nor was it necessary that he should.[23]

This parody of wifely virtues illustrates how different
the experience of marriage was for men as, literally,
opposed to women.

For the separated wife there were hardships of a
different sort. Social ostracism, exile from the family
home and relative poverty were their usual fate.
Rosina Bulwer Lytton was not cushioned from these
possibilities by her own family and neither did she
have independent means, nor the right to alimony
payments from her husband. Fortunately Edward
Bulwer-Lytton provided her with an income but it was
insufficient for her needs and, conveniently for him,
forced her to retreat to such social back-waters as
Llangollen in North Wales and then Taunton in the
West Country. Because most of the professions were
closed to women, the prospect of earning her own
living was fraught with difficulty. In her novel
subtitled *The School for Husbands* (1851) she
complains that 'men have a thousand resources from
which women are debarred'.[24] Among these are the

[23] Rosina Bulwer Lytton, *Behind the Scenes: A Novel*, 3 vols (London:
Sweet, 1854), I, p. 197.

[24] Bulwer Lytton, *A School for Husbands*, preface.

male networks ranging from the public school and the masonic lodge to the men's clubs, within which she includes the government. The social and professional segregation of the sexes enforced by these male networks allowed men to escape women's company at the same time as they consolidated and retained their power. In her novels, Rosina Bulwer Lytton ridicules men's clubs from The Garrick to The Athenaeum. In *Miriam Sedley*, a woman is symbolically situated outside the club looking in through a window at the members who 'look for all the world like a set of stuffed birds in glass-cases, and however ornithologists may dispute as to the birds, of the stuffing there is not the least doubt'.[25] In attacking the Institute of the Guild of Literature and Art that Charles Dickens and Edward Bulwer-Lytton had founded,[26] Rosina Bulwer Lytton renamed it 'The Guilt of Literature and Art'.[27] In order to make her husband feel guilty about her impoverished circumstances and, at the same time, to supplement her income, she decided to take a leaf out of his book by becoming a writer of fiction.

For this enterprise, the literary establishment not only failed to give her much support, but greeted her with considerable opposition. Recognizing that much of this antagonism was from her husband's supporters, Rosina Bulwer Lytton resolved to succeed in the literary world by playing him at his own game. She deliberately set out to trade off his success. Despite her antipathy to her married name, she did not adopt a *nom de plume* except for her final novels,

[25] Bulwer Lytton, *Miriam Sedley*, II, p. 183.

[26] See Sybilla Jane Flower, *Bulwer-Lytton* (London: Shire Publications, 1973), pp. 37–39.

[27] See Bulwer Lytton, *A School for Husbands*, preface.

and neither did she hesitate to use her title. She even wrote novels along similar lines to his and produced a less successful version of his occultist master-piece *Zanoni* (1842), echoing the name of his eponymous hero through her character, Zamora in *The Peer's Daughters* (1849).[28] Rosina Bulwer Lytton, who had already developed the art of mimicry, found in her husband's novels material with which she could develop her talent for pastiche and parody. The plagiarisms for which he was notorious must have been in her mind when she playfully plagiarized in *Miriam Sedley*, the much ridiculed opening of *Paul Clifford* (1830) 'It was a dark and stormy night'.[29] This line inspired not only Rosina Bulwer Lytton but also the twentieth-century competition run in San Jose for the worst opening of a novel. Not only does she satirize her husband's writing-style, she also lampoons him. He crops up in various transparent disguises usually as a gold-ringleted dilettante who wrote novels glorifying male villainy. In *Cheveley*, we are told that Mr Trevyllian wrote a novel called *The Unnatural Son* 'which being full of terrible things was naturally much admired'.[30] Occasionally Edward Bulwer-Lytton takes the form of a woman, as in *The Peer's Daughters: A Novel*,[31] where he is transmogrified into Madame De Pompadour, and in *Miriam Sedley*, where he appears as Lady L., who is the author of the *Philanthropic Poisoner*. His most famous

---

[28] See Rosina Bulwer Lytton, *The Peer's Daughters: A Novel*, 3 vols (London: T.C. Newby, 1849).

[29] Edward Bulwer-Lytton, *Paul Clifford* (London: Scott, 1887), p. 1.

[30] Rosina Bulwer Lytton, *Cheveley: or, The Man of Honour*, 3 vols (London: Bull, 1839), II, p. 93.

[31] Bulwer Lytton, *The Peer's Daughters*, I, p. 180.

appearance is in *Cheveley*, which boasts the ironic subtitle, *Man of Honour*. This was such an accurate portrait that it inspired a counter-attack in the form of a poem entitled *Lady Cheveley or, The Woman of Honour* (1839). Invoking patriotism, the sacred duties of motherhood and the obligations of a wife, the poem reinforces the Victorian values that its subject had rejected:

> Oh, monstrous! see the mother of his child,
> With blackest slander has his name defiled!
> And o'er his noble heart a sickness came,
> Not for his own, but for his deathless shame.
> The coarse allusion, the indecent jest,
> The falsehood half revealed and half supprest,
> And vilest calumnies profusely poured
> On the fond mother whom his heart adored.
> His sacred anguish is no theme for song,–
> But heaven is merciful! and truth is strong!
> He still could trace upon that mother's cheek
> The holy sympathy no words can speak?
> Still his spotless name to Britain dear!
> And friendship still his wounded heart can sheer!
> But his were trials which no muse may sing.
> To spare the viper, while he felt the sting!
> To know the sanctity of home defiled!
> To blush for her, the mother of his child!
> In silent pride his cruel wrongs to bear,
> To know that words could crush – and yet to spare!
> And feel that pride compelled him to return
> The loud-tongued slander with a silent scorn!
> Oh you! who, safe in ambush, aimed the dart
> Of coward malice at a husband's heart.[32]

[32] Anon., *Lady Cheveley or, The Woman of Honour*. A New Version of *Cheveley or, The Man of Honour* (London: Churton, 1839), pp. 42–43.

By retaining anonymity, the author of the poem, like the target of his attack, is 'safe in ambush', yet she, who is accused of cowardly malice, unlike the poet at least allowed her identity to be revealed. The most likely candidate for its authorship is Edward Bulwer-Lytton himself, who was suspected by Rosina Bulwer Lytton of having also been the instigator of some of the negative reviews of her books that poured from the presses of periodicals, that he patronised.

Rosina Bulwer Lytton's attempts to win sympathy in her reader and out-manoeuvre her critics, is indicated by her foreword to *Very Successful* which is addressed 'To those who understand'. In order to circumvent attacks from reviewers, she shifted her authorial voice from that of writer to editor. In the preface to *The Prince Duke and The Page* (1841), she underlines the difference on the grounds that 'nine tenths of the world agree to confound the words author and editor, into a strange *synonyme*'. This denial of agency and the taking on of a new authorial persona was a fresh tactic with which she negotiated the world of publishing. She goes on to predict that reviewers would still 'suspect that I had attempted to baffle their penetration by taking refuge in the Incognito of Editorship'. Ultimately she confounded her critics by using an anonymous publisher for her final novels *Clumber Chase* (1871) and *Mauleverer's Divorce* (1871) and writing them under the male pseudonym, George Scott.

Messages to Edward Bulwer-Lytton are encoded within her novels, where fact mingles with fiction. Their titles hold the promise of tabloid exposés: *Behind the Scenes, The World and his Wife* (1858) significantly subtitled *A Photographic Novel, School for Husbands* and the much maligned *Very Successful*. This novel came under such heavy attack that the only positive note that appeared in some reviews was the title itself. The author claimed that, as part of the conspiracy against her, provincial libraries were discouraged from accepting *Very Successful*, because it was allegedly unsuitable for ladies to read.[33] In the prefaces to her novels, Rosina Bulwer Lytton accused her estranged husband of trying to suppress her books, by threatening her publishers, printers and book-sellers. The dedication in *Cheveley* addressed to 'No one, nobody, Esq., no hall, nowhere' was intended to puncture Edward Bulwer-Lytton's self-importance. In a letter she refers to his family seat Knebworth as 'Naughtworth' – a mischievous reference to its having been heavily mortgaged because of the cost of recent alterations.[34] The description of Knebworth in *Miriam Sedley* turns out to be an uncanny omen for its author: 'it has since become a private mad-house, whereas, at that time, it was only an asylum for idiots.'[35] Knebworth is a target in her comic novel, *Budget of The Bubble Family* (1840) where she ridicules the family in residence, headed by Edward Bulwer-Lytton.

Not the first woman writer to attack her husband in novels, Rosina Bulwer Lytton compares herself to Charlotte Smith, who was separated from her husband and had to support her twelve children through her writing:

[33] Lady Bulwer Lytton's *Appeal to the Justice and Charity of the English Public* (Privately Printed, Taunton, 1857), p. 4.

[34] *Unpublished Letters of Lady Bulwer Lytton to A.E. Chalon, RA*, ed. S.M. Ellis (London: Eveleign Nash, 1914), p. 253.

[35] Bulwer Lytton, *Miriam Sedley*, III, p. 217.

...in the last century there was a novelist, a certain Mrs Charlotte Smith, who only laboured under an incipient attack of ordinary jog-trot-bad husband, and yet *she* vigorously threw out the *complaint* by serving him up – or out? – in every novel she wrote – hot, cold, *roasted* and *devilled*, and yet she was not reviled and lapidated: on the contrary, she was voted extremely clever and very much to be pitied! Then, to be sure, poor Mr Smith, good easy man, not only bore it all, but frankly owned that he deserved it, and did not set the blood-hounds after her because, under the torture, his victim had uttered a cry that reached the public ear.[36]

In this parody of Jonathan Swift's parodic *Modest Proposal* (1729) where various ways of preparing and eating babies are proposed, Rosina Bulwer Lytton suggests different ways of serving up a husband such as 'hot, cold, *roasted* and *devilled*'.[37] But unlike her prolific predecessor, she did not have an 'ordinary jog-trot-bad husband' like the obliging Mr Smith, who felt that he deserved such treatment from his wife's pen. On the contrary, Edward Bulwer-Lytton resisted and opposed his wife at every turn. One new strategy Rosina Bulwer Lytton employed was to suggest in print that if Edward increased her allowance then she would stop attacking him and even give up writing novels altogether. There could be no greater subversion of the tradition of the proper lady apologizing in a preface for immodestly putting pen to paper for such reasons as having to support her fatherless children, than Rosina Bulwer Lytton's

[36] *Unpublished Letters*, ed. Ellis, p. 84.

[37] Rosina Bulwer Lytton admired Swift's writing and he appears as a character in *The Peer's Daughters*.

blatant attempt to blackmail her husband. It would appear that he resisted her offer and so the attacks and the novels continued. In *Memoirs of a Muscovite* (1843), she parodies herself, with a touch of irony:

> Lady Craven then wrote books without the slightest allusion to her husband or his, if possible, more infamous family, but merely to make herself a little independent in circumstances, but this was precisely what his mean, cruel and calculating persecution most objected to, most dreaded, because pecuniary independence is power.... So Sir August resorts to crushing his wife's books.[38]

As Rosina Bulwer Lytton correctly points out, an estranged wife who is able to earn her living through writing can wield power which her husband and his family might find threatening. But the point at which such subversion becomes dangerous for all concerned is when the demarcation between the private and the public is dissolved and real life no longer masquerades as fiction.

Having publicized her position through the newspapers, Rosina Bulwer Lytton went even further, by appealing directly to the public for funds in a pamphlet entitled *Lady Bulwer Lytton's Appeal to the Justice and Charity of the English Public*. Here she denounced her husband as 'a literary Cagliostro, political Titus Oates and marital Henry the Eighth'.[39] With this threefold attack on him as author, politician and husband, she tried to humiliate him into increasing her allowance. It is ironic that Rosina Bulwer Lytton had declared politics to be a 'national

[38] Bulwer Lytton, *Memoirs of a Muscovite*, I, p. 167.

[39] *Lady Bulwer Lytton's Appeal*, p. 4.

Juggernaut'[40] under which everyone is sacrificed since the effect of her *Appeal* and public opposition to her husband meant that not only had she thrown herself at the feet of the public, but also under the Juggernaut itself. From that point on, the weight of the establishment slowly began to crush her. There were rumours of an attempt to poison her and a plot to steal her papers. The crunch came when Rosina Bulwer Lytton fly-posted Taunton with notices to the electorate condemning as 'Sir Liar' her husband, who had recently been appointed Secretary of State for the Colonies. While he was canvassing in Hertford for nomination as a Tory Member of Parliament, Rosina Bulwer Lytton then made a speech urging the electors not to vote for him. For a cabinet minister, member of the government and electoral campaigner, the embarrassment must have been acute. Regarding these actions as tantamount to insanity, Edward Bulwer-Lytton decided to have his wife committed to a private lunatic asylum. On 21 June 1858, two doctors certified her as insane and confined her, against her will, in Inverness Lodge in Brentford.

By the middle of the nineteenth century, the number of women incarcerated in both private and public asylums outnumbered men. This was partly due to the law that decreed in 1828 that asylums must have medical supervision. The Lunatics Act of 1846 reinforced the claim of the medical profession. The result of this legislation was that the care of the mad resided in the authority of a body of exclusively male professionals. Perceptions of madness changed once it came within the purview of the doctor. Now insanity was believed to be of somatic origin, emanating from

[40] *Loc. cit.*

the brain, and a manifestation of an organic illness rather than a disorder of the mind, the emotions, or spirit. These changes which had accompanied the transformation of the mad-houses of the previous centuries into the lunatic asylums of the nineteenth century had significant implications for the admission and treatment of women.[41] For them the asylum was a site of moral management where women's minds were controlled by the restrictions imposed on their bodies. Within middle-class society, the limitations placed on women had increased the incidence of nervous disorders. Medical literature confirmed the view that women wanting to cultivate their minds put at risk not only their reproductive organs, leading to sterility, but even their sanity. Women who rejected the restricted role of femininity were seen as resisting nature and therefore unnatural, while deviations from lady-like behaviour were pathologized by the medical profession. In his case history of Rosina Bulwer Lytton's committal, Thomas Mulock, despite his sympathy towards her, still maintained that her action was 'manifestly wrong and discreditable *on the part of a lady*' [my italics].[42] To his way of thinking, a wife should be loyal to a husband however he might mistreat her. Public speaking, particularly when it consisted of an anti-husband diatribe, was considered to be behaviour not fitting for a lady. The cure was drastic, since Rosina Bulwer Lytton was committed to a lunatic asylum, where she was restrained and

---

[41] See Roy Porter, *A Social History of Madness* (London: Weidenfeld, 1987), pp. 103–24, Phyllis Chesler, *Women and Madness* (Harmondsworth: Penguin, 1979), Ussher, *Women's Madness*, pp. 63–94.

[42] Thomas Mulock, *British Lunatic Asylums Public and Private* (London: Tweedie, 1858), p. 48.

effectively silenced. However, the publicity that she had generated during her campaign ensured her release after three weeks and rescued her from the possibility of long-term incarceration. Hot-tempered like her mother and Irish grand-mother, her reaction on release must have been of seismic proportions. If Edward Bulwer-Lytton had expected reform or acquiescence he was much mistaken.

The most explosive permanent after-effect was the publication of *A Blighted Life*. Written in 1866, it was not published in book form until 1880, seven years after Edward Bulwer-Lytton's death. Its appearance may have been timed so that it could join forces with Georgiana Weldon's *How I Escaped the Mad-Doctors* (1878) which was also a protest against the right of husbands to contain rebellious wives. Three years later, Louisa Lowe produced *The Bastilles of England; or, The Lunacy Laws at Work* (1883) on the same subject.

The existence of *A Blighted Life* is evidence that the attempt to contain Rosina Bulwer Lytton failed. The text represents her ultimate rebellion because of its opposition to male power and privilege. Outspoken attacks are made here on the literary and political establishment from the public schools which turn out 'underfed and over-birched boys'[43] to the cabal of gentleman and politicians. Such questions are posed as 'But how *could* this country be anything but the Land of Cant and Crime it is, when we see the irredeemably infamous men who occupy the highest places in literature and politics in England at the present day?'[44] The way in which this power is

[43] Bulwer Lytton, *A Blighted Life*, p. 3.

[44] *ibid.*, p. 5.

retained and abused, she argues, is through a
freemasonry of gentlemen which ensures that 'each
gentleman's vices should be held sacred by any other
gentleman, as there is no knowing when their own
turn may come'.[45]   Referring not only to her *own*
situation, but also to political irregularities which she
regarded as examples of corruption, Rosina Bulwer
Lytton attacks the establishment as an 'infernal
Machine of occult power' which no man would dare
'*explode against himself* to save any woman from
being incarcerated in fifty mad-houses and
bechameled afterwards in minced meat, as small as
that which Puss in Boots threatened to cut the
reapers'.[46]   Not even Queen Victoria is exempt from
her scorn and is blamed for rewarding Bulwer-Lytton
with a peerage instead of supporting, in sisterhood,
his long-suffering wife in her grievances against him.
Rosina Bulwer Lytton did not have a high opinion of
the monarch, whom she describes her as 'our little
selfish, sensuous, inane and carnal Queen [who]
would not care if all her subjects were equally
distributed in Madhouses, or pounded in mortars'.[47]

Elsewhere in her fiction she had sought to shift and
displace her authorial persona through a variety of
characters, both male and female. But in *A Blighted
Life* both the narrative voice and the targets of her
attack are made explicit. Because of this, the
consequences of its publication were disastrous. Its
appearance in the public domain disrupted the private
life of the author. Since Edward Bulwer-Lytton was
no longer alive to defend himself, what may have been

[45] Bulwer Lytton, *A Blighted Life*, p. 9.

[46] *ibid.*, p. 4.

[47] *ibid.*, p. 42.

intended as a vindication of his wife who had survived him could be seen by its critics as vilifying the dead. This is probably how it appeared to her son Robert, thus making a reconciliation between them impossible. To make matters worse, the new Earl of Lytton reacted to the perceived outrage against his father by reducing his mother's allowance in circumstances where she was already vulnerable to a ruinous suit for libel. Rosina Bulwer Lytton insisted that the text had never been intended for publication in the form in which it appeared but that a copy had been made without her knowledge and published without her consent. The reason why it had been written in the first place had been as source material for a report being prepared on the contemporary state of asylums. This explanation is upheld by her loyal biographer, Louisa Devey.

In an attempt to pacify her son and those who were on the verge of bringing law suits against her, she wrote a pamphlet called *Refutation of an Audacious Forgery of the Dowager Lady's name to a book of the Publication of which she was Totally Ignorant* (1880). This satisfied her son sufficiently for him to reinstate her allowance in full. Even though the title of the defence is so explicit, it is misleading, since the content does not deny that Rosina Bulwer Lytton was the author of *A Blighted Life*. The purpose of the pamphlet is to insist that she was not responsible for its publication and that it had never been intended for wide circulation. *A Blighted Life* contains little that had not already been hinted at in her previous publications. The only difference is that here the names had not been changed to protect the guilty. For this oversight, and for transforming into a main narrative of explicit disclosure material that had been presented to the reader in the past in the disguise of fictional sub-plots, digressions or asides in her novels, Rosina Bulwer Lytton literally paid dearly.

The text is open to a number of interpretations. It may be read as the hysterical outpourings of a manic-depressive which might provide French feminists with a sample of psycho-babble from the semiotic chora. Anglo-American gyno-critics are likely to approach it as a record of a woman's protest against patriarchal oppression. It is ironic that Rosina Bulwer Lytton had wanted her life-story to be edited by two men. What we have instead is a raw document that represents the uncensored and unrestrained voice of a Victorian woman. The text even escaped her own efforts of self-censorship since she claims to have colluded in bringing about its suppression. It is the rare expression of a woman's outrage and indignation in extraordinarily difficult circumstances, particularly in her conviction that she had been forcibly deprived of her children.

Her subversive writings and demand for public attention succeeded in breaking the conventional silences that had traditionally surrounded domestic and marital disputes. In doing so, she disrupted the phallocratic order in which a woman's identity is fashioned by her relationship to the male world. Marriage was the anvil upon which this was forged. Rosina Bulwer Lytton's campaign to break her chains had an adverse effect upon her husband. She must have been a considerable thorn in the side of Edward Bulwer-Lytton, who ironically had once wooed her with a rose-bud. Louisa Devey claims in her biography, that it was Rosina Bulwer Lytton's dearest wish that after her death, an attempt would be made to clear her reputation. But instead of achieving this, the appearance of *A Blighted Life* had the opposite effect in some quarters. It hardened the bias of biographers like Michael Sadleir against her and alienated the Bulwer-Lytton family from her for several generations. In 1971 when David Lytton Cobbold (now Lord Cobbold) was preparing the Edward Bulwer-Lytton Centenary exhibition at Knebworth House, he decided that it was time that Rosina should be rehabilitated as his ancestress. He hung her picture at Knebworth for the first time and called his daughter, who was born in December of that year, after her. So one hundred years after the death of Edward Bulwer-Lytton's wife her family have accepted her back in the fold.

Rosina Bulwer Lytton's determination never to give up her fight for vindication and revenge is signified by the title of the last novel she wrote; *Where there's a Will there's a Way* (1871). Resilient to the last, she had proved herself to be indefatigable, for as the unsympathetic and acerbic biographer, Michael Sadleir pointed out; 'the daughter hardened into a permanent replica of her mother, becoming and remaining a feminist as wrong-headed and as tedious as ever had been the Goddess of Reason herself'.[48] Rosina Bulwer Lytton's grand-daughter, Constance Lytton inherited her intrepid spirit to the point of heroism. Feminist writer and militant Suffragette, her civil disobedience led to her being imprisoned and force fed for the cause of women's suffrage. In their different ways, Anna Wheeler, Rosina Bulwer Lytton and Constance Lytton subverted their prescribed roles

[48] Michael Sadleir, *Bulwer and His Wife: A Panorama 1803–1836* (London: Constable, 1931), p. 81.

whether they be that of daughter, wife or mother. All three escaped either the institutionalized prison of marriage or triumphed over the physical incarceration of the asylum and gaol in the fight for the freedom and equality of women.

Nowadays, out of these three women, the one we know least about is Rosina Bulwer Lytton. As she was neglected towards the end of her life, so she was neglected in death. It is significant that the grave-stone and inscription she had requested in her 'Last Will and Testament' had been denied her until recently and that her writings have been out of print for over a century. Unfortunately she was never able to complete her autobiography nor the text based on her own life called *Nemesis*, before she died. Apart from her fictional autobiography *Miriam Sedley*, the only memoir that survives in full is *A Blighted Life*. Reprinted here for the first time in book form,[49] it should be approached as a narrative of protest and not used as a yard-stick by which to judge her writing. For that the reader should turn to her novels. The importance of *A Blighted Life* is that it did draw attention to the wrongs suffered by married women and the abuse of asylums as a means of containing troublesome wives; but whether it succeeds as a vindication of the life of Rosina Bulwer Lytton is for the reader to decide.

Marie Mulvey Roberts
Bristol, 1994

---

[49] I would like to thank Helen Boden, John Charles Smith, Charlie Butler, Marion Glastonbury, Michael Foot, David Cobbold, Sibylla Jane Flower and the staff working on the archives at Knebworth House for their invaluable help and advice in the preparation of this edition.

WORKS BY ROSINA BULWER LYTTON

Cheveley: or, The Man of Honour, 3 vols (London: Bull, 1839)

The Budget of the Bubble Family, 3 vols (London: Bull, 1840)

The Prince-Duke and the Page: An Historical Novel, 3 vols (London: Boone, 1841)

Bianca Cappello: An Historical Romance, 3 vols (London: Bull, 1843)

Memoirs of a Muscovite, 3 vols (London: Newby, 1844)

The Peer's Daughters: A Novel, 3 vols (London: Newby, 1849)

Miriam Sedley, or The Tares and the Wheat: A Tale of Real Life, 3 vols (London: Newby, 1850)

The School for Husbands: or Moliére's Life and Times, 3 vols (London: Skeet, 1852)

Behind the Scenes, A Novel, 3 vols (London: Skeet, 1854)

Very Successful!, 3 vols (London: Whittaker, 1859)

The World and his Wife, or a Person of Consequence, a Photographic Novel, 3 vols (London: Whittaker, 1858)

The Household Fairy (London: Hale, 1870)

Where there's a Will there's a Way (published anonymously in August 1871 by Bacon)

Clumber Chase by Hon. George Scott (published anonymously, 1871)

Mauleverer's Divorce by Hon. George Scott
(published anonymously, 1871)
Shells from the Sands of Time (London: Bickers,
1876)
A Blighted Life (London: London Publishing Office,
1880)
*Refutation of an Audacious Forgery of the Dowager
Lady's name to a book of the Publication of which
she was totally Ignorant* (Privately printed, 1880)

A BLIGHTED LIFE.

BY THE

RIGHT HON. LADY LYTTON.

A True Story.

WITH THREE ILLUSTRATIONS.

London:
THE LONDON PUBLISHING OFFICE,
3, Falcon Court; 32, Fleet Street, E.C.
1880.

ILLUSTRATIONS.

PREFACE.

"THE BLIGHTED LIFE," by the Rt. Hon. ROSINA, Lady LYTTON, with the Supplemental Notes which seemed necessary to make it complete, is now presented to the world in a perfect form; and the Editor hopes, that as it is one of the most interesting, so it will prove likewise one of the most useful of books. It details, in a highly graphic manner, a narrative of persecution of the most base and unmanly kind, practised by a wicked Man of great talent and resources, upon a Noble Lady, who had hardly anything to defend her but a high spirit, a consciousness of innocence, and a resolve not to be crushed. This man had all the help that Power, and the Plots of guilty Associates could give him; he was himself false, cruel, cunning, and unscrupulous; and yet he was foiled by Lady LYTTON, alone and almost unaided, except by the Voice of Public Opinion, which conquered the devices of both Court and Cabinet—for we believe that each was implicated in this most foul transaction.

The Volume contains Three Portraits; one of Lady LYTTON, which is now for the first time given to the world; but which hardly does justice to her beauty, intellect, and grace: a Portrait of her husband, highly flattered; for almost every low and evil passion was traced indelibly on that odious countenance; and it was impossible to look upon him for any time without feelings of disgust and even horror: the third is that of her Son, the present Lord LYTTON, on whose conduct in this business we forbear to comment; we leave the consideration of it entirely to the public.   As the handwriting of Nature developes in the features, the eyes, the forehead, and the mouth, the true character of the soul and spirit within, we recommend a careful contemplation of these Portraits to all students in physiognomy, and think they will find, as they examine, a confirmation of their own best experience in this most interesting branch of science.   Lord LYTTON the First hid his mouth with his moustache and beard, because he was too conscious of its frightful expression to let it be seen.

The most saddening thought that arises after the perusal of this Volume, is, that no change has yet been made in the infamous Lunacy Laws, for which, in the main, we have to thank our Whig Rulers.   Never was a more criminal or despotic Law passed than that which now enables a Husband to lock up his Wife in a Madhouse on the certificate of two medical men, who often in haste, frequently for a bribe, certify to madness where none exists.   We believe that under these Statutes thousands of persons, perfectly sane, are now imprisoned in private asylums throughout the Kingdom; while strangers are in possession of their property; and the miserable prisoner is finally brought to a state of actual lunacy or imbecility—however rational he may have been when first immured.   The Keepers of these Madhouse Dens, from long study in their diabolical art, can reduce, by certain drugs, the clearest brain to a state of stupor; and the Lunacy Commissioners take all for granted that they hear over the luxurious lunch with which the Mad Doctor regales them.

Let us hope that this Volume may again call public attention to the monstrous crimes that are perpetrated under this dreadful system; and that it may help to unrivet only one of the brazen fetters which now bind down our People in bondage.

The character of the main Figure in this Volume has been often drawn in flattering colours—most usually, we fancy, by his own descriptive pen.   He has been called Poet, Novelist, Orator, Statesman, and we know not what; but if his Wife's Narrative, as contained in these pages, be correct, he was assuredly about as complete a Scoundrel as ever walked in shoe leather.   And that the Narrative is strictly accurate and absolutely true, we entertain no doubt whatever.   And if so, how odious was his conduct to that injured Lady. We believe that the man who would immure a perfectly sane Wife in the prisons of a Madhouse would not hesitate at her murder, if he thought himself safe. And it was in that horrible crime that Lord LYTTON was detected, and fortunately was foiled. How well we recollect the universal horror which the news of the deed occasioned. *The Daily Telegraph* was then on its last legs. It had hardly a circulation of 3,000 a day. As each new morning dawned we expected to hear of its death. In a happy moment for the LEVY-LAWSON-LEVIS, Lady LYTTON was betrayed, seized, and immured. The Editor saw his chance, and made the Metropolis ring with the outrage. LEVI was saved ; so also was Lady LYTTON. She was released, as described in "THE BLIGHTED LIFE ;" but to the horror and indignation of all decent people, her betrayer and most brutal torturer was nevertheless retained in office as Colonial Minister by the QUEEN, who, soon after, in order to mark her high sense of his conduct, elevated him, and his equally-infamous brother HENRY, to the peerage. A more shameful insult, either to the People or to the House of Lords, was never committed; but insult now seems to be the lot of us all, and so VIVAT REGINA !

A BLIGHTED LIFE.

THE following is a true Woman's Record of sad suffering. Her wrongs have driven her half mad, and we do not wonder that it should be so, for she has sought redress in vain from almost every source. Her trampler and her tyrant was always victorious in every conflict. The QUEEN, as she most usually does with all criminals, took him by the hand; petted, favoured and promoted him; while his Victim was driven from Society into poverty and exile, and was for years the unceasing object of abuse, slander and libel. God pity her! May God protect and avenge her! Excuse her language, O Reader, whenever it seems "strong," for it is the cry of an indignant and broken heart—it is the wild shriek of Right, crushed under the heel of insolent and guilty Might.

SIR,—Time was, ere I grew too sick of fiction, or rather of the hollow unprincipled *vaux rien*, who for the most part trade upon it, that your and THACKERAY'S works were the only *novels* that I read; because they were the only ones independent of their indisputable talent * that bore the Hall mark of sincerity, and of conveying the real feelings and opinions of the writers; and not written up to the market standard, whether the twaddle was to be about very little children, which costs nothing—on paper—or underfed and overbirched boys; to say nothing of that great charm, that intellectual aroma of their being written by educated

* *Genius* was written originally, but was obliterated, and *talent* substituted for it.

B

gentlemen. But your Novel I have not read, having a horror of all things that emanate from or appear under the auspices of that patent Humbug, Mr. CHARLES DICKENS, or any of his clique, and it is only the having seen in the " Englishwoman's Domestic Magazine " for this month, a review of your Novel, and an extract of your Notice, and requesting all persons in various ranks of life, who by letter or *viva voce*, during the last five years have told you of some persons incarcerated in asylums, &c., &c., &c., and inviting fresh communications, &c, &c., &c., which induces me to furnish you with a few additional facts as to the incarceration—villainy—so much in vogue. But don't mistake my motive in so doing. *I want you to do nothing for me ;* for nothing can *now* be done, and if it could, *je connais mon Angleterre trop bien* not to know that the English to a man are *the* most sordid, selfish, time-serving tuft-hunters in the whole world; Mammon being their only god, and Self high priest: and moreover I am also too fully aware, after 25 years' bitter experience, that wherever the literary element enters, there *cameraderie*, expediency, clap-trap, treachery, moral cowardice and concrete meanness are *sure* to follow. There *is* such a thing as cheap chivalry, as well as cheap philanthropy, which are the only sorts *à la porte de Messieurs les litterateurs Anglais.* And it makes all the difference in the world to make a *cheval de bataille* (and become a hero upon it) of a poor man's wrongs, who has *no* powerful foes to bring their masked batteries to bear upon his champion—aye, or in the event of the victim's being a chimney sweep's wife—for the *same* reason there is nothing easier than for chivalry to make a desperate and victorious onslaught upon Soot, as psychologically as well as horticulturally that pulverised darkness would only make the laurels flourish the more luxuriantly. But change the venue and let the victim only be in the upper sphere of life, without father, mother, or *money*, while her infamous husband not only having with his brother done dirty work for *every* government for the last 30 years, and being moreover a *litterateur* whose grossly immoral plagiaries had been be-puffed by a venal press as immortal works, for value received in government interest, and invitations to their vulgar wives— shew me the man in England who would move a finger that might make this Infernal Machine of occult power *explode against himself* to save any woman from being incarcerated in fifty mad-houses and *bechameled* afterwards in minced meat, as small as that into which Puss in Boots threatened to cut the reapers, and to save the lurch of your *true* motto.

Dict sans faict,
A Dieu deplait.

The Chivalric Philanthropist in question would immediately

and most conveniently feel that "no man had a *right* to interfere between another man and his wife, as this, of course, came under the category of strictly private and family affairs." To say nothing of the *real* gist of the matter, to wit the Freemasonry which exists among "gentlemen," (?) that each gentleman's vices should be held sacred by any other gentleman, as there is no knowing when their *own* turn may come. So the non-intervention plan is by far the best, alias the safest, both for Parliamentary and Philanthropic humbug. How well my meanest of all villains, and most unlimited of all blackguards knew this, when years ago, after one of his brutal outbursts of personal violence, the cowardly reptile said to me: "*Remember, Madame, you have neither father nor brother, and therefore you are completely in my power.*" When, 23 years ago, I and my then infant children were turned out of our home, to make room for one of this loathsome brute's then strumpets, Miss LAURA DEACON, Serjeant TALFOURD had just cooked up *his* sham popularity-catching Custody of Infants' Bill. A silly friend of mine persuaded me to send my case to him, as one of the *strongest* and *most flagrant* that could possibly be. I pointed out to her that he also wrote Plays and Poems; and knowing what utter blackguards you "literary men" are in this country—for as old LANDOR says, "there is a spice of the scoundrel in them all"—and therefore *he* was not likely to risk either the puffery or the persecution of that literary political ruffian. And I was the Cassandra as I always am, for the "learned Serjeant" kept my papers a few days and then returned them to me, saying, "he was very sorry he had not *time* to look at them." A pretty person to bring a Bill into Parliament, who had not *time* to look into the most flagrant abuses that necessitated the change in the law. True, GOD's judgment overtook *this* hypocrite at last; for he who *never* went to bed sober, after a most eloquent diatribe against drunkenness the Bacchanalian Judge fell back stone dead, instead of *a son ordinaire* dead drunk. But how *could* this country be anything but the Land of Cant and Crime it is, when we see the irredeemably infamous men who occupy the highest places in literature and politics in England at the present day? Men whose triumphant vices and poisonous example are enough to breed rottenness in the very marrow of the nation. And they *have* done so; more especially their impious hypocrisy. When GOD was on earth the *only* sin he had *no* mercy on was hypocrisy. And why? Because it is a rank and blasphemous forgery on Heaven. When the late Sir ROBERT PEEL wanted to make Lord LYNDHURST Lord Chancellor, he could not do so because of the £15,000 unpaid damages hanging on him about his crim.-con. with Lady SYKES, whereupon Mr. BARING, the present Lord ASHBURTON said, "I'll pay the damages for COPLEY if you'll give me a peerage," and this *creditable* guardian of the public morals (which, of *course* are only preserved by private debauchery) had not been six months Lord Chancellor before he had another crim.-con. with Lady G., during the trial for which, poor Lord G. cut his throat. But he, the moral cause of the tragedy, lived to concoct at the instigation of one of *the* most infamous of our extensive aristocratic Traviataocracy, MESSALINA NORTON, our present job Divorce Court, and to die, puffed by a venal press as if he had been a saint or a demi-god. Faugh! how sick it all makes one. Then see we not still living, to false-weight the scales of justice, that other precious legal DON JUAN and doer of dirty work *dessous les cartes*, for his old college chum, the Chief Justice Sir ALEXANDER COCKBURN, who, as DENISON, the law reporter of the *Times*, said the other day, was "about the most unprincipled scoundrel in England," passing his whole time in debauching the wife or daughter of every man who came in his way. So with all this *Diabolus ex machina* up the *backstairs*, like the onions in SYDNEY SMITH'S salad, "unsuspected, animating the whole," you may imagine the fearful odds a poor legal Victim with "neither Father, Brother, nor Money" has against her! But never mind, "wait for the end." *Dieu et mon droit*, and the indomitable hatred and colossal contempt of them *all* with which I am nerved makes me feel that, single-handed and alone as I have before partially been, I shall yet effectually be more than a match for these immund reptiles. This is a long Proem, but it was almost necessary to make you comprehend this of necessity condensed and therefore not over-clear because not categorical *résumé* of such a tissue of complex and chronic iniquity before coming to the culminating atrocity of Sir ——'s mad-house conspiracy; which, beyond the details you have *asked* to be supplied with from all quarters, of course can have no earthly interest for you, who once truly remarked in a note I received from you, that "for the most part the fine feelings or rather fine sentiments of Authors were all fused in their inkstands for general circulation, which left them none for their own personal use." And yet verily, I think LAMARTINE is right, when he says, "*Si l'on savait tout on ne serait indifferent a rien.*"

To begin at the beginning of the Mad-house Conspiracy episode, for the Ruffian long ago began his lies in Paris, having put an infamous libel in his lick-dust *ame damnée*, the *Court Journal*, about my having insulted his brother at a ball at Lady AYLMER'S, to which Lord AYLMER had forbidden the brother to be asked, and to which, therefore, he was *not* asked. For this gross lie and libel, my solicitor, a Mr. —— ——, *then* and ever a red-hot Tory, instantly brought an action against Sir ——'s tools, as Sir L. *then* called himself a Whig, and got me for my counsel Sir F. POLLOCK, the present Chief Baron. The defence the dastardly wretches set up in court was that *I* had fabricated this gross libel against myself, to bring myself before the public!!! Whereupon my counsel remarked that even in a Court of Justice I was not free from the base calumnies of my unscrupulous enemies. *Bref*, I gained this action, costs and damages against them, but pray bear in mind the name of my (as I thought) devoted attorney, Mr. ———— ————, who, as the sequel will show, was only a devoted and unscrupulous jobber to the Tory faction. Well, as I said before, to begin at the beginning of the Mad-house Conspiracy episode, I had taken a cottage in the Fulham-road in 1852, but being very poor I was obliged to furnish it by degrees, and after the drawing-rooms and library, had only furnished my own bed-room and dressing-room, when, with my usual good luck, a most—to me—loathsomely disgusting person, from her extreme personal dirt, hideousness, and inanity, came down to me crying one cold wet November day, saying her relation, Mrs. LOUDON (Mrs. CORN-LAW LOUDON, who says COBDEN stole all her fame from her), had literally turned her into the streets, that she had not a *sou;* knew no one in London but me, who she thought would have compassion on her, and both her brothers were away. What could I do? Had I had ready money to pay for a lodging I would have done so ; but I had not a farthing till a publisher's (of the name of SHOBERL) bills for between £400 and £500 became due. Then my poor pretty furniture, among which I would rather have let loose a whole litter of pigs! Oh! it was a horrible dilemma ; but not being made of stone cemented with mud, as I ought to be, with the infamous name I had the irreparable misfortune to be branded with at the matrimonial galleys, I gulped all my difficulties and disgusts, and sent for an upholsterer in hot haste to furnish at a year's credit a bedroom (which should have been a sty for this biped swine), and as my intention was to let my cottage whenever I left town, there was no use in furnishing it less well than the rest of my little gem of a house, which I had done cheaply enough, picking up the things by degrees for ready money. Alas, in one week the housemaid came to me with tears in her eyes to come and see the wreck ; and truly the Augean stable must have been the *beau ideal* of neatness and cleanliness to it. The honest creature stayed with me a year in my poor cottage, I finding her not only in evening dresses, but in clothes from head to foot, as I did for three years after in other places, being, of course, therefrom obliged to do without essentials for myself. At the end of that year, my swindling publisher, SHOBERL, went smash, and I did not get a penny ; but the obliging upholsterer came down upon me with an exorbitant fancy bill for the furnishing Miss R——'s room, more in amount than any three other rooms in the house. I really felt stunned, or rather crushed, as if an elephant had trodden down my heart. I was for four months ineffectually trying to let my cottage, and as ineffectually (tied up as I was on a beggarly pittance of £400 a year for that monster's life, irregularly paid) trying to borrow money. At length a good Samaritan at the Stock Exchange, a stranger of course, and his good, excellent unattorney-like lawyer, poor Mr. HODGSON, now also dead, said he had heard such a good character of my honesty from the best judges, or at least the most impartial ones, the creditors, that he most humanely and generously lent me £1000 at £5 per cent. for 10 years, and paying £100 a year off the principal, and insuring both Sir —— 's and my own life. With this fearful drain upon my already disgraceful pittance, as you may suppose, I could not stay in London. My friends, by way of economising, asked me to go on visits to them; so I went first to Lady HOTHAM at Brighton, and then to other friends there, but soon found out that there is nothing *so* expensive as visiting in great houses, and dressing and going out, &c., &c., &c. So after a short trip to Paris with Lady HOTHAM, I went to bury myself in a little village in Wales (Llangollen), where the people about the country were good enough to come and see me, but I honestly told them I could not afford to go and see them, as I was even obliged to give up my maid, which to me was indeed a bitter, bitter privation. Then it was, being at a village *inn alone*, that that cowardly brute Sir —— thought he had *beau jeu;* and sent down first a vulgar old woman calling herself Mrs. P—— with her " darter" and one of Sir —— 's bastards (of whom I could give you an incident quite fit for a novel, but too long to insert here), the said P—— scraping an acquaintance with me upon the plea of her being an American, which she acted to the life by obtruding herself upon me at all hours, breakfast and dinner, and in my bedroom before I was up of a morning, and of course she had as good a right to be in the *hotel* as I had. One day, before I came into the dining-room, she had helped me to soup. I found her with her bonnet on, and before I had time to eat the soup, she pretended she had had a sudden summons to London and was off. I had no sooner eaten the soup than before dinner was over I was seized with the most agonizing pains and violent retchings. My Doctor gave me antidotes; and said some attempt had been made to poison me, but the dose had not been sufficient. This seemed to be confirmed by my (in about three weeks) getting a letter from old P—— (*which letter I have got*), with another from another old adventuress, calling herself Mme. S——, who, being at K—— with some more of Sir —— 's elegant acquaintances, says she overheard · the whole plot to incarcerate me in a Mad-house, and so have me *gradually* made away with. She also sent me a copy of a letter, which she says (?) she sent to Sir ——, after I *was* incarcerated, saying if a hair of mine was injured she would denounce him publicly as the black villain he was. Well, to return to old P——'s letter. In it she seemed seized with a remorse of conscience—her grandchild having died suddenly, and that she was off to Paris, but could not go without *warning me* " for GOD'S sake to be upon my guard, as a person would be sent down whose name would begin with G, and to attract my attention, in order to scrape acquaintance with me, she would have a little black King Charles dog," *as old P—— herself had had.*

Before I come to the spy No. 2, Miss G——'s arrival, I must tell you of three other personages in this infamous *dramatis personæ.* Soon after my arrival at Llangollen, a man calling himself " Mr. LEIGHTON," and purporting to be a theatrical manager, wrote to me for permission to dramatise my novel of ——, which I gave him; but this correspondence extended over so many months without anything being done, his letters being dated Theatres Royal, Southampton, Birmingham, Liverpool, Manchester, in short, every provincial theatre in the kingdom, that I, of course, began to see this was some fresh villainy of Sir ——, who, after cutting the ground from under me in every unimaginably mean way, by preventing my earning the bread he will not give me, no doubt thought it a rare jest to fool me into the supposition that one of my books, which is a ready made drama, was going to be dramatised. But one has only to look at his hideous face, and that of that other brute, DICKENS, to see that *every* bad passion has left the impress of its cloven hoof upon their fiendish lineaments. However, as HAYDON the painter told old MELBOURNE years ago, " Any scamp who trades in politics is considered a fit companion for Lords," and my Lord DERBY seems to have a *foible* for most unprincipled and disreputable scamps, and such adventurers as D—— and Sir —— are admirably calculated for ' Nyanziang' at our exceptionally stupid and inane Court, before our Royal BETTY FOY, " the idiot mother of an idiot boy."

But to return to Llangollen. I luckily kept all the *soi-disant* Mr. LEIGHTON's letters, and the Llangollen post office was kept by a druggist of the name of G—— D ——, while *next* to his shop was a gin shop kept by a *very* low person of the name of J——, who had formerly had something to do with minor theatres and had narrowly escaped transportation for some of his malpractices. He and this D—— were great cronies, and a private door in a passage of J——'s gin-shop *opened into the post office department of D——'s shop.* Bear all this in mind. This J—— was then living with the maid of a woman with whom he had formerly intrigued, and whose whole family he had ruined. Well, as soon as I got old P——'s letter of warning, I put all the people of the ' Hand Hotel' on their guard, and as it was then the depth of

winter, no tourists came to Llangollen, and I told them to be *sure*
and let me know if anyone whose name began with a G came to
stay there. About ten days after this, BRELLISFORD, the waitress,
came to me, and said an old woman looking like a housekeeper
had just arrived from the station to take apartments for "her
young lady," a Miss G——, who had just lost her mother, and
who intended to spend some time at Llangollen. BRELLISFORD,
who had been by me put in possession of old P——'s letter,
answered her sharply that it was very strange that a young lady
who had lost her mother had no friends to go to, but should come
to such a desolate out-of-the-way place, to which the old woman
made no reply. I then told BRELLISFORD to let me see (unseen)
this old woman, and to be *sure* and let me know when the
young lady arrived. Soon after B—— came up in haste
to say the old woman was going to the Post, and that
I could see her from the window. I ran to it, and who
should I see but old TATE, Sir L——'s housekeeper ! ! ! The
young *lady* did not arrive till two nights after ; a most hideous
vulgar-looking creature, past 40, with a fiery red face. The morning after her arrival, old TATE left in haste for London, telling Mrs.
P——, the woman of the Inn, that she had a large dinner to attend to. For six mortal days Miss G—— was unable to fire her first
shot, for even old P——'s old King Charles "Tiney," who had been
re-christened " Prince " for the new campaign, had only succeeded
in getting a snap from my Blenheim Tiger on the stairs, unac-
companied by his mistress. For I was waiting for the enemy's
first move before I opened my batteries. It appears that the very
first day at dinner, so well acquainted was she with *the carte du
pays* from her predecessors, that she accosted the waitress by her
somewhat uncommon name of " BRELLISFORD," asking her to
carve a chicken. " Pray," said the latter, " how did you know
my name ? " Miss G—— coloured and stammered and said she'd
heard her called so. " That you havn't since you've been in this
house, for all the servants call me SARAH." On the seventh day,
instead of resting from her labours, the amiable G—— could
hold out no longer, and *apropos de bottes* asked BRELLISFORD at
dinner " If I never went out ? " " Seldom in the winter," was
the reply. " Dear me," said Grogblossom, returning to the
charge, " I wish Lady —— would take a drive with me."
Though of course the vulgar wretch, *a la* DICKENS, said " ride."—
" Not very likely," said B., " after that *other* (emphasising the
word) vulgar old Spy of that bad man, Sir —— ——, Mrs. P——,
playing up the games she did here, Lady —— is not likely to let
any more, *no one knows who*, force themselves upon her." " Spies,"
re-echoed Grogblossom, " dear me, what can he have to spy her
about. Every one knows what a profligate bad man he is ; but
at all events, I am not in a sphere of life to know Sir ——

EDWARD, LORD LYTTON.

—— as an acquaintance, and I'm far too respectable to do his dirty work." "Then," said BRELLISFORD, firing up as she snatched the last dish off the table, "if you are not in a *spear* of life to know Sir ——, who is just fit for the likes of you, how dare you presume to ask, or to think, that her ladyship would go out with you?" and slamming to the door, with an excellent imitation of thunder, she hurried down the passage, and came to my room to report "that Miss GET-NOTHING'S," as she always called her, impudence, and tell me the whole conversation. Whereupon, I instantly wrote a short note saying that if Miss G—— did not take herself off *instantly* to her infamous employer, I would have her forcibly ejected. This note I took *myself*, and, opening the door, flung it *without going in*, on the round table, in the middle of the room. A *full* quarter-of-an-hour after she got up a series of screams, doing duty for hysterics, and rang the bell violently for Mrs. P——, telling her that I had insulted her (G——) in the most violent and unprovoked manner, and that I must be *mad* (*c'etait la sa consigne*). Old P—— came to me in great consternation, saying, "I should not have taken the law into my own hands." "You never mind that," said I, "but go back and tell her that if she does not leave this to-morrow morning, I'll find a way of making her; and if she feels herself aggrieved, and don't know what to do, I'll tell her—namely, if she is *not* a Spy of that Cowardly Ruffian, Sir ——'s, sent to finish the job old P—— begun, let her instantly go to her lawyer, and instruct him to bring an action against me for defamation." Mrs. P—— returned in a very short time to say that Miss G—— had said very *humbly* she *would* go as soon as she possibly could; but she had come in such a hurry she had had to buy a flannel petticoat!!! on her arrival (*idem* old P——'s *darter*, to whom the same romantic incident of travel had happened), and that she must write for *money* (ditto old P——'s "darter" again), having none, and she could not possibly get an answer before the day after to-morrow.

Now Sir —— was at that time flaring up at Leeds, lecturing at Mechanics' Institutes upon "The Holiness of Truth" to the "snobs," and the Sacredness of Probity!! till, as a lady who wrote me word of it said, she wondered the earth did not open and swallow the blasphemous monster. I told SARAH BRELLIS-FORD to be sure and bring me any letter or letters that came to Miss G —— on the morning she expected the *indispensable* remittance, *not* to open or destroy them, or intercept them, as her friend Sir —— would have done; but merely to see the superscription, that is, the handwriting of the remittance letter. Well, it came, with Sir ——'s unmistakable mean scrawl, and *crest* on the seal, and the Leeds postmark, *and no mistake*, and two hours after Miss G—— was bundled off. She was scarcely gone when I got

letters from London imploring me to be on my guard, as these
G——'s lived at Brighton, and the one sent to Llangollen *had a
carriage always ready on the road, in order, if I could be found out
walking, to kidnap me, and carry me off to a Madhouse*, as Sir ——
was giving out all over London, *via* a Mr. ROBERT BELL, one of
the DICKENS's literary clique, that I was *quite mad*, and also by
his infamous *ame damnée*, the infamous attorney, L——. Now
this L——, you must know, Sir —— himself told me years ago,
" *intrigued with his own sister, to save the expense of a mistress !* "
A fitting tool, truly, for so loathsome a ruffian as the bran new
baronet! And the attorney boasts with his sardonic grin, " Oh!
Sir —— ——, he *must* do whatever I please." After I had put
Miss G—— to flight, I wrote to Lady HOTHAM and several others
at Brighton, to find out who and what those G——'s were, and
telling them of the Madhouse Conspiracy *en train*. To which I
got back an ocean of English twaddle and conventional cant,
telling me not to talk of spies and madhouse conspiracies in the
19th century, but to remember that I lived in a *free* country
(very *free*, for any villainy to be practised with impunity, where
there is money to pay for it, a position to cover it, or Lords
PALMERSTONS, DERBYS, LYNDHURSTS, or Chief Justice COCKBURNS,
who so long as they do the *public* humbug well in verbal sound-
ing brass, can and do employ the most infamous tools to do their
private dirty work, and of course are in duty bound to *screen* and
protect the said tools in all their own little personal crimes and
enormities), and above all, I was told to remember that however
bad Sir —— might be, he knew the laws of his country, and
couldn't (couldn't he, when it is done every day !) incarcerate me
without a public (oh, dear) and full enquiry about all my
sayings, and doings, and habits, which would be the very *best*
thing that could happen to me, as he had so many years ground
me down to poverty, as to effectually make me a dead letter ; so
that all the lies he so indefatigably disseminated about me went
by default. However, as one evening Lady HOTHAM was
repeating at dinner the sapient advice that she had written to
me to her Brighton Doctor, a Dr. T——, who lives in Regency-
square there, and another gentleman, an acquaintance of mine,
Dr. T—— said, " G——, G——! Stop; I *do* know some
people who know two Miss G——s. My wife and I are going
to a party there to-morrow night, and I'll try and find out what
I can about those Miss G——s." " Do," said the other gentleman, "and as I must return to town to-morrow, be so good as
to write and let me know what you do find out, that I may tell
Lady ——, as I don't at all agree with Lady HOTHAM about the
madhouse conspiracy being a chimera of hers." Accordingly,
the day after the party, this gentleman received the following
letter from Dr. T——, which he sent me, and which I have got.

It began : " Dear Sir,—I went to the party I told you of last night, and sure enough who should be there but a Miss G——, who was boasting that Sir E—— L—— was a great friend of theirs, and that her *sister* had just returned from Llangollen, where she had seen that horrid wife of his (a lie, for she had *not* seen me), who was quite mad, but she was happy to say also, so ill, that she could not live a week. Poor Lady L——, it is really too hard," Dr. T—— goes on to say—but I need not trouble you with the rest of the letter.

The summer after this I got out of the hotel into a lodging, small, but very nicely furnished, of which I took the whole *except* the parlours, which, as the woman only asked 25 shillings a week for them, I told her on *no* account to let them to any one, but if she had an offer to do so I would pay her for them rather than have any other lodger in the house, after all I had suffered. Nothing could exceed the attention and *prevoyante* civility of these people. But when I had been there about three weeks, to my great horror and indignation, in the teeth of her promise, she informed me that she had let the parlour to a lady and gentleman, as they had given her two guineas a week for them ; this alarmed me more, whereupon this silly woman, to re-assure me, told me she was a lady of the highest connections, a Mrs. B——, as she herself had told her she was related to Lord This and the Marquis of That. I said, my good Mrs. P——, depend upon it by her giving you more than you asked for your rooms, and bragging about her great relations, she is not a gentlewoman, but some improper person or other. The next morning the plot began to thicken, and up came a great disgusting dish of *raw* trout with Mr. B——'s compliments, as he had been out fishing, though Mrs. P—— let out that he had bought them of Mrs. J—— at the gin-shop. I returned them saying I was much obliged, but I never ate river fish. Through the windows I had the felicity of seeing Mr. and Mrs. B——. He looked a something between a retired undertaker and a methodist parson in a rusty black coat and a dirty white cravat and shoes and stockings of a morning ; and she was a perfect hybrid (with long black ringlets, a staring silk Stuart plaid dress, and very short petticoats) between a ballet girl at a fifth-rate theatre and a Regent's-street social evil, who did *not* attend the midnight meetings. I have since heard from indisputable authority that these vulgar wretches are always with Sir —— at K—— and Ventnor, and elsewhere, that he took to intriguing with that raw-boned frau, Madame ERNST, and dedicating his Balderdashiana in ' Blackwood ' to her paralysed gorilla of a husband, ERNST the fiddler, whose society must be delightful to a man who is as deaf as a post, and who, before he was so, in point of music did not know " BOB and JOAN" from " GOD save the QUEEN," and who does not know *one word* of German. For of all his literary charlataneries, his pretended translation of —— —— was the most iniquitous, as at them it was he slaved his poor young daughter to death. His French is execrable and ridiculous enough; still he can read and understand it, though he does call naïveté *navelty!!* which is almost as marvellous a travesty as that other woful attempt at an admirable CRICHTON and an omniscient genius (?), Mr. W —— R ——, who calls VOLTAIRE—VOLL-TAIRE, so as to rhyme with NOLL; and who seems strongly to confound notoriety with fame, and therefore went to the trouble and expense of going to Africa to so *usefully* enlighten the world by informing it that when he attempted to kiss the African young ladies, they ran away! Why—he need not have gone so far to make that discovery, as " my dear husband to a toad-stool " (which is a fair bet, the venemous reptile against the poisonous fungus), had he made the experiment in England every young lady, to a crinoline, would have done the same. This singularly antipathique young gentleman who, after favouring me with a brisk correspondence which I knew must have some covert meaning, as an Englishman *never* does anything without a sordid or selfish motive, last June did me the honour of inflicting upon me a three days' visit, ostensibly *en route* to Tenby to see his parents, of whom he spoke in a depreciating contemptuous manner that quite disgusted me, as if, poor silly people, they were quite below par, and unworthy of having such a son—I beg pardon, such a genius (?) of a son. With true English good breeding he hunted me up the day before I could possibly receive him, but however stupid he might have been to me, I daresay it was agreeable enough to him; as I understand he spent his nights down in the bar, which I should think was a much more congenial place to him than a drawing-room. When he went, as I thought, to Tenby, he wrote me word he had gone back to Oxfordshire, " and his parents would keep," as upon getting to Reading he found he had no money! This was so very like all the Sir ——'s innumerable myrmidons, that it gave me as I wrote a cold shudder; as I could not but solve the mystery of his correspondence and invasion by setting him down as one of Sir ——'s spies, in which idea I am confirmed by his after getting or not getting what he wanted, just like a true English boor, and with his insane literary mania and evident absence of principle, I have no doubt he would be glad to ingratiate himself with that infamous man on *any* terms. A friend of mine suggested to me as a solution of his visit, that perhaps he had heard that I was such a fool, as the dear, selfish English say, in helping others, when I so sorely needed help myself, that he might have wanted to borrow money; but though

I may be able to skin myself in £20 or £30, he surely could not suppose that any one condemned to the miserable and disinherited life I lead could have any hundreds to lend him towards ministering to his overweening and senseless vanity? I have not seen his book, feeling no interest in it after seeing him; but I was silly enough two or three years ago to give him a volume of Essays that I had written in great haste, thinking he might sell them for a few pounds; and I should not be the least surprised if every thought in them (originality certainly not being his forte) were, *a la* Sir L——, made to do duty as his reflections in "Savage Africa." The kissing episode I have quoted was sent me by a lady in a newspaper extract to make me laugh, which it did most heartily. Now to return to the dear B——, whom I understand with the Swiss drab of a governess whom Sir —— seduced long ago at Malvern, and whom recently in that pretty —— trial about the crystal ball he improvised as his cook! thinking, no doubt, that as the devil sends cooks and also concubines, it was all the same thing, and cook sounded better in a Court of Justice. So these B——s and the Swiss Traviata form the *corps d'armee* of his spirit-rapping establishment, which is this great man's mode of combining spirit and matter: the vice being the *real*, and his genius the *ideal*, or *non est*.

Well, Mr. B——, I suppose by way of doing his spiriting gently, that is, not disturbing the spirits (except those in the brandy bottle, to which he gave no quarter, but always full measure), used always to take off those pretty dust undertaker's *shoes* of his to steal up and down stairs, which I suppose meant that if I was going out of the drawing-room I might not be deterred from doing so by hearing a step upon the stairs.

A few evenings after I had returned the trout caught in the lake of *Gin*-eva down at J——'s, the evening being very sultry, I was obliged to leave my drawing-room door slightly ajar, when, to my horror, who should come tripping in with a basket of strawberries but the social amateur evil, dressed, or rather undressed, to a pitch that would have alarmed even an art student. She made me a sort of theatrical speech in which she introduced herself and her strawberries. I never eat strawberries any more than trout; and in the absence of Wenham-lake ice, my reception of her must have been most refreshing, or rather refrigerating. Nothing daunted, this intensely vulgar piece of effrontery (who, I understand, is a natural daughter of that horrid old scamp, Lord LOWTHER: hence her high connexions) spread her furbelows, and, uninvited, seated herself; and seeing the shoeless undertaker creeping upstairs, she had the crowning impertinence to call him in, and introduce him to me, I visibly petrifying the while, and not replying to a single thing he said; till the he

B——, by way of saying something pleasant, remarked that DICKENS was a wonderful man. "A wonderful brute and humbug he certainly is," said I. The she B—— then began, with a volubility that reminded one of one of CHARLES MATTHEWS'S patter songs, to recount to me a spirit-rapping story of an umbrella that had been left in a corner, and suddenly took it in its head—its ivory dog's head at the end of the handle—to turn round, walk across the room, and walk downstairs; whereupon I said in an insinuating voice: " *Will* you both have the goodness to show me how it went downstairs?" At which Mr. B—— indulged in a loud guffaw, and gently and elegantly knocking his two thumbnails together, as if he had been trying vivisection on a flea, said, "Not bad; not bad." I then rose, and very stiffly announced that I had drank tea, was going to bed, and could not offer them any wine and water, as I never drank wine; whereupon this "charming woman," turning briskly to the undertaker, said, "B——, run down, and bring up the wine and spirits." I said, "Not here, pray,". and darting into my bedroom, locked the door.

The next day came a note from Mrs. B——, expressing her great sympathy with all I had suffered; and as the cuisine was not particularly good at those lodgings, would I do them the favour of dining with them at the hotel? I sent down a verbal message to say that I never dined out. The next day the pair took their departure for London; but the people of the house became suddenly and unbearably insolent; and although I had taken the rooms for six months certain, said I must leave them *immediately*, as they had let them. This was pleasant, for lodgings are difficult to get at Llangollen, and worse than that, it wanting six weeks to the time I should receive my parish allowance, and also to the time when the two months' rent would become due, I had not a *sou* wherewith to meet this sudden and unfair demand in the teeth of a written agreement. But my kind old Dr. PRICE not only came to the rescue, rating these vile people soundly, and telling them they would repent their shameful conduct before they were much older (which they did), but he kindly got me another lodging higher up in the same road, in which I had not been installed a week when Dr. PRICE wrote to me, saying that horrid woman Mrs. B——, and a woman she called her maid, were installed in my old lodgings. I put on my bonnet and went out to pass the house, and what should I see but Mrs. B—— and her *soi-disant* maid sitting on the *sill* of the open drawing-room window, with a salver between them with two decanters of wine on it, and glasses in their hands, over which they were laughing and singing; and as soon as they saw me they set up a perfect shout.

Two nights after this, the lady and her maid were literally

drummed out of the place for roaring and screaming about the streets with men, at between one and two in the morning, and disturbing the quiet village. So Mrs..P—— and her brother did not get much by their infamy to me, and to their highly connected Patroness Mrs. B——, more especially as I lodged a complaint of their conduct with the Baptist minister, who lectured them publicly in chapel for it. A fortnight after Mrs. B——'s expulsion, Mr. B—— came down solo, and went to the Chester races, in an open carriage and four, with those two blackguards, J—— of the Gin Shop, and D—— of the Post-office, driving past my windows, shouting and roaring and waving their hats ; and previous to his departure, B—— wrote me a most infamous anonymous letter, beginning that "he had the QUEEN's and ——'s permission to sleep with me"—which letter was *precisely* in the same hand-writing as all those purporting to be from Mr. L——, the *soi-disant* Theatrical Manager, *which infamous letter, and all the rest*, I have got. Upon this crowning outrage inflicted by that far more ruffianly B——'s myrmidons, I sent for Mr. WHALLEY, the Magistrate, the present member for Peterborough—(Maynooth WHALLEY), and he told J—— he would take away his licence. I, of course, could not stay in a place where I had been so outraged and persecuted ; and then it was I wrote to a friend of mine to engage me rooms in some Hotel in this dead-letter town ; and sending all my luggage on to London, directed to a Mrs. WILSON, for her to forward them *here;* I took a young person who used to make my dresses at Llangollen as my maid, coming on here without any luggage but a carpet bag with " passenger " on it, so that none of the Llangollen people knew *where* I was going, by which means Sir —— completely lost the track of his victim, which made him so furious that when good Mr. HODGSON went to receive my pittance, as he always did, Sir —— and the ruffian L—— vowed they would not pay it till they had a clergyman's certificate ! to say I was alive ! which was, of course, as they thought, a clever plan to find out *where* I was ; but Mr. HYDE, my solicitor, whose country place was at Sangport, 16 miles from this, and who was then alive, and had not *yet* found his account in selling me " *to screen the party,*" wrote to say, that if my beggarly pittance was not instantly paid, Sir—— should have the best of all assurances that I was *alive*, as he, Mr. HYDE, would drive down to K—— with me to take possession, and remain there with me to protect me. So the dastardly brute was foiled for the nonce. Soon after I came here Miss R—— again was homeless, and gave me the benefit—no, the discipline—of her company, and worried me into sending a statement of my case to Lord LYNDHURST, who was then, with MESSALINA NORTON, concocting the job of the Divorce Court. Apropos of the latter, she is such an awful hypocrite, quite of

Sir ——'s calibre, that they would have made a matchless pair, because she is actually a *proverb* for brutalising servants and governesses. I see in to-day's *Times* she has a long and charmingly benevolent letter advocating the cause of Poor Servants against their not sufficiently considerate masters and mistresses! Oh! why does not the Devil foreclose his mortgage upon those three such hypocrites, Mother NORTON, Sir ——, and DICKENS, and drive them and their fine sentiments round his dominions. Sir —— at least would not be quite new to the lash, as years ago, when that infamous Mrs. NORTON kept her amateur house of ill-fame in Bolton-row, and Sir —— was intriguing with a cousin of hers, a Mrs. BARTON, the wife of a clergyman—some "good-natured friend" wrote to Mr. BARTON and told him if he would go at such an hour to Mrs. NORTON'S, and walk up into the back bedroom, he would find Sir —— with his wife. He did so, and horsewhipped Sir ——. Whereupon MESSALINA, putting her arms akimbo, said, "If you are such a d——d fool that you cannot manage a little affair of this sort without being found out, you must go elsewhere." The uninitiated keep wondering how the *Examiner* could puff that intensely trashy and immensely infamous last book of Mrs. NORTON'S. But those who know that she used to intrigue with that hideous old ALBANY FONBLANQUE, and any other dirty editor that came in her way, for a puff, don't wonder at all. If any of Mrs. NORTON's ill-used servants were to write to the *Times*, illustrating by a few *facts* her practical benevolence and consideration towards them, I should just like to see the *Times* printing *them*, though thanks to our wheel within wheel of Humbug within Humbug, and Sham upon Sham, the *Times* can do its cheap brummagem philanthropy and championship of the oppressed as well as any other "Tartuffe" in the kingdom. And yet this most vile woman (with plenty of others of the same sort) is received at "our Virtuous Court," and quite worthy of being so, by the little selfish sensuous Inanity who rules over it, the Murderess of poor Lady FLORA HASTINGS, and the *amiable* daughter who did all she could to hold up her own mother with Sir JOHN CONROY. Poor excellent Prince ALBERT, a *rara avis*—a man who *had principle* and acted up to it, from the smallest to the greatest things,—knowing neither truckling nor *expediency*, had a life of it! happy he to have so soon escaped, and gone home to a more congenial sphere, where he invested the great treasure of *good deeds*, while still a labourer here.— But to return to the LYNDHURST affair : I told Miss R—— that my sending my case to Lord L—— was like writing in water; nothing would come of it. Still, I drew it up as briefly as I could, with a full statement of the last Llangollen infamy; but fortunately I was obstinate in my own common sense and would not yield to the *sapient* Miss R——'s advice to send him some infamous letters of Sir R——'s, which he, the ruffian, has denied on oath! For what are perjuries to one who has lived upon them as MITHRIDATES did on poisons, till they have become his daily food? Neither did I send him any original documents, beyond my own written statement of facts. So well am I aware, with regard to the thimble-rig of Politics, of what *my* fate would be, no matter who were the *ins* or the outs. I told Lord LYNDHURST *not* to take the trouble of writing, but merely make his secretary acknowledge the receipt of my papers till he returned them with his opinion. But two months passed and I had no acknowledgment of even the receipt of the packet. I then wrote again, expressing my surprise at this, when I received a note from Lord LYNDHURST, beginning, "My dear lady L——." Cool, from a man I did not know personally. This is the note—

"My dear Lady L——, In the hurry of business I mislaid your *present* address, and therefore wrote to you at Llangollen, telling you that I had read your papers, and written my opinion on them, and that they were left with my porter ready for you whenever you sent for them. Ten days after I had despatched my letter to you, a young woman called at my house, saying she had been sent by Lady L—— for her papers, and my porter gave her the packet addressed to you. Therefore I was much surprised on the receipt of your letter this morning, saying you had *not* received the papers.—Believe me, yours faithfully, LYNDHURST."

In reply to this "Strange Story," before Sir L——'s other blasphemous "Strange Story," that that brute DICKENS just published, I wrote to Lord LYNDHURST to say that in the first place I never should have sent in that vulgar, cavalier way, without writing a note to him for my papers; in the next, it was strange he should have forgotten my *present address!* and only remember my former one at Llangollen, since BOTH addresses were *equally mentioned in the papers he said he had left with his porter for me.* But that such being the case, it behoved him for his own honour (?!) to stir in the matter, and find out who had got the letter he wrote to me at Llangollen, out of the Llangollen post-office, and who the woman was who had called for the papers, with the infamous lie that I had sent her. And the first step towards this was to tell the date of the letter he had written to me, and the day, and then the office in London at which the letter had been posted; and next, to employ Mr. PEACOCK, the Solicitor of the post-office, to sift out the affair, as, like a true-born Briton, he of course would be likely to put more zeal into his measures if employed by Lord LYNDHURST to detect an affront and fraud practised upon *him*, than merely an outrage and an injustice practised upon me, or every other defenceless woman in England. To this I received a *palpably* shuffling and wide of the mark note from Lord LYNDHURST, and the farce was gone through of writing to that vile fellow D——, at Llangollen, who actually had the effrontery to pretend that no such letter had ever arrived at Llangollen post-office for me. Then *how*—as I told my Lord LYNDHURST, *could* the swindlers who called for my papers have known where to do so, but for the information contained in that letter? unless, indeed, the letter *was a myth*, and his lordship, to make things pleasant to *the party*, had kindly made over my papers to my Lord DERBY's creditable Colonial Secretary? which was the only other *possible* solution of the affair. D—— then wrote to me, " did I suppose that after my great kindness to his poor wife, in her last illness, which he should never forget, that he could do anything to injure me?" To which I replied yes, that was the very reason why he would; as I had never yet served anyone, in much, or in little, that they had not repaid me by the basest ingratitude, treachery, and injury—of some kind. My Lord LYNDHURST, finding I would *not* be quiet, though the old Tory jobbing attorney Mr. C—— H——, under the pretence of setting Mr. PEACOCK to work, but in *reality* to seize the golden opportunity of scraping personal acquaintance with an old Tory law lord, and by joining issue with him, to make things pleasant to the *party*, and crush and gag their victim a little more. So, finding that I was not the plastic, swallow-anything Fool that men think women ought to be, and which for the propagation and comfortable impunity of their vice, too many women are, my Lord LYNDHURST sent down his nephew and private secretary, Mr. RICHARD CLARKE, to see what he could do in the much-ado-about-nothing-humbug line. I boldly taxed him with this Divorce Bill being a job concocted between Lord LYNDHURST and Mother NORTON. "Well," said he," you put it in such a point blank way, that I cannot deny it." You can, if you like, said I, or anything else, but I'm not bound to believe you. I then taxed D—— with having a finger in the pie with regard to the swindle of my papers; knowing the creditable way in which, years ago, his acquaintance with Lord LYNDHURST (which was his first political stepping stone, after poor fool of a WYNDHAM LEWIS had paid his election expenses at Maidstone) had begun, namely, by their joint property with three more in Lady SYKES. "Oh," said Mr. CLARKE, "D—— and Lord LYNDHURST are two. D—— has not crossed our threshold for ages; and we all nearly fell off of our chairs laughing at breakfast, the other morning, at the capital, and to the life facsimile you gave in that imaginary conversation you put into his mouth, in your last letter to Lord LYNDHURST." But Mr. RICHARD CLARKE could do nothing with me, for I assured him this disgraceful affair should *not* rest between Lord LYNDHURST, me, *and the post.* I then, as a *pis aller*, got General THOMPSON to present a petition in the House of Commons demanding an inquiry into the fate of the papers sent to Lord LYNDHURST, of which I could obtain no *clear* or satisfactory account. The poor superannuated Conservative peer, from his place in the House of Lords, mumbled some circumlocution rubbish about his being the last man to be guilty of want of courtesy to a lady.—Hang his courtesy!! his justice and common honesty were what I wanted, and not his courtesy; but it is precisely those two exotics which are not to be had in this accursed land of crime and cant, and so this infamy ended in smoke, as most things do in the two Houses of Humbug down at Westminster. I need not tell you, from the day I ordered her out of Llangollen to this, *dear* Miss G—— never brought any action against me. No doubt your Orthodox English Conventionality is greatly shocked at my "coarse," "violent," "unladylike language"! But you must make some allowance (though English people never do, being wisely and justly only shocked and scandalized at terrible results, while they remain perfectly placid and piano upon terrible *causes*); but I was going to say you must make some allowance for a person writhing under nearly life-long, unparalleled, everrecurring, and never-redressed outrages,—and suffering from a chronic indigestion of falsehood, hypocrisy, and unscrupulous villainy. No wonder, then, that the other day I cordially sympathised with a man who said, that though no more fires blazed, or faggots crackled in Smithfield—for which thank GOD—he should like to make a bonfire of all the fine benevolent sentiments DICKENS, Sir EDWARD LYTTON, and Mrs. NORTON ever wrote, with those of that other scoundrel LAWRENCE STERNE, and placing the three former within smelting heat of the flames, collect an equivalent quantity of ink to all they had ever used in gulling the public, and force the black-lie-vehicle down their throats! It was this same man who wittily said, constituting himself *Advocatus Diaboli*, when a whole room full of people were crying out against the utter trash and horrible immorality of Mrs. NORTON's last book—" Well, now, I like the book, for it may be considered as Mrs. NORTON's oral confession, her *peccavi*, in fact, as it so clearly and abundantly proves that there is not a single *Traviata* 'dodge' in all Babylon that she is not *practically up to.*" Which sally was received with peals of laughter, and "Hear, Hear's."—Talking of the humbug and omnipresence of *Self* in Authors, how thoroughly characteristic was that vainglorious " *In Memoriam* " of poor THACKERAY by Mr. DICKENS in this month's *Cornhill;* it being a mere stalkinghorse to parade his own importance and repeat the compliments poor THACKERAY had paid him, though there were so many other and better things the public would all have rather heard of *good*

THACKERAY. It was also a way of letting the groundlings know that his son, Master DICKENS, had been at Eton, though he took good care not to tell them that Miss BURDETT COUTTS had paid for him there. For she can do these supererogatory display things, and build churches, though she cannot give a private *unknown* guinea to her own starving relations, of which, like everyone else, she has some. I liked Mr. TROLLOPE's " *In Memoriam* " much better, and from the extracts I have read from his wishy-washy vulgar Novels, I did not think he could have written so well. Only I wish he had not opened with that tag Latin quotation ; for though Latin is all very well, and indeed at times necessary for terseness' sake to add force to sense or satire, *real* feeling generally finds expression in our mother tongue.

After this LYNDHURST swindle of my papers, Miss R—— went to her brother, who was then in London : this was in the autumn of 1857. The part Mr. H—— had acted on that occasion first raised my suspicions against him : but alas, what is the use of a prophetic spirit, when one has nobody to help one ? That is no visible earthly help ; and no wonder if long before this time I had reversed the injunction to fear GOD and love my neighbour, for I love GOD more and more however much bitter wrong He may for some inscrutably wise purpose allow, but I fear my neighbour most " consumedly." Sir LIAR had of course found out my new abode by the LYNDHURST conspiracy, so the creature lost no time in being at his dirty work again. Accordingly, towards the end of October I was brought up a card with " Mrs. S—LL—" upon it, accompanied by a message that the lady (!) wanted particularly to see me. I enquired where this lady came from, and was told she had just arrived from London by the train ; had engaged a bed here, but had not a vestige of luggage, or any servant with her. I told them to say I was not well enough to see any one ; and to repeat that answer while she remained ; and that whatever business she wanted to see me upon she could state in writing. I then told them to send Mrs. C—— to me ; and when she came I begged of her to watch this woman narrowly, as I strongly suspected she was some fresh Spy of that infamous wretch Sir L. The next morning Mrs. C—— came to report herself, and said she was sure she was some "infamous baggage," by her theatrical manner ; and saying that she would get a divorce from her husband, if she knew where he was ; but she did not know whether he was dead or alive, or anything about him (*that* there could be no doubt of), that she had come here to teach music and give theatrical readings, for which she wanted to hire Mrs. C——'s ball-room, which Mrs. C—— refused to let to her ; she then asked all sorts of questions about me, and said, she *must* see me. Mrs. C—— coolly told her that the word was rather inappropriate. She then, it appears first by bribery, and then by bullying, sought to make the chamber-maid tell her the number of my *bed*-room, and to give her a room next to it; upon which the chamber-maid very nearly insulted her, but thought it better to trick her instead, so took her to a room on the second floor, and quite in another wing of the house. The next morning she returned to the charge of trying to see me, and gave her a *written* prospectus of all the great masters who had taught her singing and the *harp*, and all the great people whom she had taught; but in this list I did not fail to remark that both the teachers and the taught were all conveniently dead; this and the mention of the harp brought a sudden conviction into my mind *who* the *soi-disant* Mrs. S—LL— really was, especially when Mrs. C—— talked of her exceeding vanity about her personal appearance (though now an old woman), and above all about her hand, and when I asked for a personal description of her, and the inventory given was the pale hay-coloured hair, faded blue eyes, and aquiline nose, I felt sure that she was no other than the *soi-disant* Mrs. BEAUMONT, *alias* Miss LAURA DEACON, for whom I and my children had been turned out of a home: who had with some half-dozen predecessors been the mistress of Colonel KING when he lived at Craven Cottage, Fulham, and who, when he discovered the game she was carrying on with Sir LIAR, turned her off; however settling £200 a year upon his poor deformed eldest child by her, GEORGIANA—which £200 a year I was told was *all* she had to live upon; as Sir LIAR with his usual generosity (!) *now* gave her nothing; though when he kept her in his fine Pompeian house in Hill-street, and the wretch dared to take my name (as she did after at petty German courts, which was done by her monster Keeper, of course, not only to insult but to defame me), a bill of £300 for a grand piano came in to me from D'ALMAINE, that this wretch had had; for which blunder poor D'ALMAINE made me every possible apology. You will see precisely *why* I bore you with all these details. When I told Mrs. C—— my suspicions, she said she would get her out of the town as soon as possible, but first warn the tradespeople about her, or she might run up bills in my name as part of her instructions. "Do," said I, "for I understand she never pays any one." Mrs. C—— did so—therefore she did not succeed in hiring the assembly or any other rooms for her *readings*, or getting any pupils. And Mrs. C—— insisted upon her leaving this hotel, which she did; going to Weston-super-Mare, but forgetting to pay her hotel bill here, which she has never done to this day. About three weeks after Mrs. C—— brought me word that she was still at Weston, teaching singing in the boarding school of a Miss R——, but that Miss R—— had said she knew this Mrs. S—LL— to be a woman of such character that she would not be seen in the street with her. No wonder English misses are what they are, when this is a specimen of English schoolmistresses. Upon hearing this I set off to Weston to call upon this Miss R——, and asked her if it was true that she had said so? She replied, "Yes—I certainly did say so." "What," cried I, starting up with indignation, "you dare place a woman about the young girls confided to your care whom you *know* to be so infamous that you would not be seen in the street with her? Shame, shame upon you." "Oh," said the "genteel" Miss R——: "I only do it for their singing, she teaches in such a very superior manner to the provincial teachers, and can teach them so much more." "Of *that* I have no doubt," I said, leaving Miss R——'s room, and house. I then went to Rogers's hotel to see if they knew anything about her, and Mrs. Rogers said she had slept there one night, but that Mr. Rogers had turned her out the next morning: and that there was a Mr. and Mrs. S—— staying in the hotel, Mr. S—— being a solicitor and a most dissipated man; and that one day he met the waiter on the stairs carrying up Mrs. S—ll—'s card to Mrs. S——, and that he (Mr. S——) took the card off the salver, and looking at it said, "Pooh! pooh! Mrs. S—ll— indeed, come, tell her that I know who she is, and not to presume to try it on by attempting to scrape acquaintance with my wife." Having gained this additional information, I went to Whereat's library, where seeing her programmes for a reading from the ' Lady of Lyons,' I wrote under her name, "*alias* Mrs. Beaumont, *alias* Miss Laura Deacon, *maitresse en titre* to Sir E—— B —— L—— and half a score more," and I told Arthur Kinglake, the Weston magistrate, he had better warn the tradespeople about her, as she paid no one. He said she was already in debt all over the place. About a week after this I was favoured with a letter from a pettifogging solicitor in Bath, a Mr. P——, upon the part of Mrs. S—ll—, to say that if I did not instantly send her £50, she would bring an action against me for defamation. To which I replied she must be aware that no one having the misfortune to be dependant upon Sir E—— B —— L—— ever had £5, let alone £50, at their disposal; but as for the action, the sooner he brought it the better: only according to my knowledge of English law, the little *contretemps* of Mr. S—ll— being lost or mislaid, might render it a difficult process. However, after several more applications for the £50, I was duly served with a summons to appear in the Queen's Bench at the suit of Mrs. Maria S—ll— " she having obtained the permission of Sir E—— B—— L—— and Mr. L—— to bring the said action." But not a word about Mr. S—ll—. I wrote to Mr. Henry H—— in London, Mr. C—— H ——'s brother and partner, to put in an appearance for me; Mr. C —— H —— being conveniently ill at Longport. I was obliged to employ a little reptile of an attorney of this town of the *name* of T—— (by the bye he has a niece, a young lady of 18, *qui chasse bien de race*, for she has just b.en distinguishing herself in divers cases of shoplifting, and stole a valuable casolette of Lady TAUNTON's at the recent ball given to Captain SPEKE). I now saw that my best card would be to send him to London to that profligate attorney Mr. S——, who said he knew all about her, and ascertain beyond a doubt her *real* name. But Mr. H——, ever alive to the interests of the Conservative party, telegraphed in hot haste for this Mr. T—— to go to him ; and no doubt to give him his lesson in the particular trickery and chicanery required to foil me and protect the party. I can only hope that where he is now gone, his fidelity may be rewarded by meeting many distinguished members of "the party" who will there be able to thank him *warmly!* Well, the reptile T—— went to town, and his report was that Mr. S—— had said, "Well, I first knew her years ago, when I was articled to old BICKET. She used to come to our office about a deed of annuity for £200, that a Colonel somebody was settling upon her, and was a lovely young creature then." "But her name, her name, Mr. T——," I broke in. "Oh, her name," said the wretch, biting his lips and his ears burning scarlet, "why I—a—that is—I ascertained *positively* that she *is* a married woman, but I quite failed in finding out her name"!!!!!

"Do you take me for an idiot," said I, "that you *dare* trump up such a clumsy, bare-faced lie ? Your instructions have been to *sell* me, in order to screen that unprincipled blackguard Sir E—— L—— and the ' party,' and therefore not to divulge his infamous mistress's name to me, forgetting in your shallow craft, that of all things marriage requires identity, and that you *could* not have positively ascertained that this creature was a married woman, which you know she is *not*, and yet have failed to find out in what name she was married "!! After muttering something about my being so sharp upon him, the wretch pretended to be highly offended, and rushed out of the room. For truly says ALFONSO KARR, *On ne peut avoir de plus grand tort, que d'avoir raison contre tout le monde. Et moi, j'ai ce grand tort là, et on ne me le pardonne pas.*

This contemptible fellow did not again make his appearance till three days before the sham action was to come on. "Let me advise you, Lady L——," said the wretch, "to try to stop it by buying off Mrs. S—LL—'s solicitor. I'll manage it for you for a £5 note." "In the first place," said I, gulping down my rage, and trying to be calm, "I think £5 more than all the attorneys in England body and soul are worth. In the next place you and Mr. H—— must really think my folly quite commensurate to your and his knavery and to Sir E—— L——'s infamy. But tell

him, or tell both of them for me, that were this room piled with
gold up to the ceiling, and I was suffocating under it, I would
not give a single coin of it to play that ruffian's game, and write
myself an ass, to have it said *I* had bribed them to stop a sham
action that they can never bring."

" Oh well, if you *won't* be advised by your solicitor" —— " I
never asked your advice, I employed you to do my work, and like
most of your tribe, you have done the Devil's instead, and sold
me—but I won't sell myself to please you." No sooner did the
special pleader in London see the citation to the Queen's Bench,
when I sent it up, than he said, "Lady L—— is quite right;
this bears farce and fraud upon the face of it "; and accordingly
the day *before* S—LL— *v.* L—— was to come on, the suit was with-
drawn. What a pity I did not oblige them by buying it off;
and what could that charming injured man Sir E—— L—— do,
but incarcerate such a wretch in a madhouse, which is the only
safe place for wives not wanted, and who *won't* and *can't* be
fooled ?

Remarkably true as far as that loathsome brute Sir E——
is concerned, is JEAN PAUL'S assertion, that the past and the future
are written in every face, for what a fiendish past and what a hellish
future are written in that worst bad man's face. HOTTEN wrote
to me the other day saying that in the memoir of THACKERAY he
is bringing out, THACKERAY'S feud with Sir L—— is alluded to,
but it is stated it was subsequently arranged; but it is not all
clearly told *how*, and could I give him any particulars on the
subject? I said I could not, and that I had always respected
THACKERAY'S loathing of and utter contempt for the charlatan
and arch hypocrite, as he had never personally injured or offended
THACKERAY, who only honestly detested him for his unredeemedly
infamous life, and the intense meanness of his nature. I had
never heard of any intercourse being effected between them,
but if there had been any such jobbed up, no doubt the *vau-
rien* venal literary clique to which he belonged had concocted it
(most likely that blackguard DICKENS). Well, after the S—LL—
affair, the ruffian tried his old plan of starving me out by not
paying the beggarly pittance he professed to give me, though he
had been warned by friends (if he has any, for though plenty
of *cameraderie*, there is and *can* be no friendship among the
wicked) and foes, not to drive me to extremities. " Truly," says
RICHTER, " the devil invented seeking and his grandmother waiting," and I was nearly worn out with both. The month of June,
1858, had arrived, and the Hertford election was to take place
on the 8th, a Wednesday, I think. The Sunday before I was
in bed with one of my splitting headaches, from ceaseless worry
of mind and want of rest. I got up, and in a perfect agony
prayed to GOD to direct me, to send me some help in my

cruel, cruel position. I went back to bed exhausted, and the
sudden thought struck me, I would go to the Hertford election,
and publicly expose the ruffian. Aye; but how? I was penniless, and three quarters in Mrs. C——'s debt. Never mind; she
was a good woman, and I did put her goodness to the test. I
rang for her and said, " Mrs. C——, I am deeply in your debt;
but I want to get more into it. I want to go to Hertford, and
publicly expose that monster; you must lend me the money to
do so, and come with me, for I cannot go alone; it is your only
chance of being paid. I know the dastardly, cowardly villain
well; public exposure is the only thing his rottenness fears. For
as long as I can beggar myself in rascally lawyers, whom he can
always 'manage,' or trust to the timid, and imbecile milk and
waterings of *soi-disant* friends, who are in reality my worst
enemies, and rivet the wrong their pusillanimity succumbs to, the
Fiend only laughs at me and them." " Very well," said she,
" I'll do it." " Then, like a good soul, you must do more. I want
some giant posters printed, to placard all over the town of Hertford, with simply these words:

" ' Lady B —— L —— requests the Electors of Herts to meet
her at the Corn Exchange this day, Wednesday, June 8, 1858,
before going to the Hustings.' "

But I told her not to get them done at a common printing
office, so as to have it talked of all over *this* town. She said
she'd have them done at the private printing-office of my chemist,
whom she could trust. On the Tuesday, by the 3.20 p.m. train,
we started, but instead of going the direct way by London—for
fear of meeting Sir LIAR or any of his gang—we went a round
which, with the usual delays of the trains, made it 11 at night
before we got to Bedford; so that the *last* train for Hertford
had started half-an-hour before, and it was three mortal hours
before post horses could be got for love or money; which threw
us out dreadfully, and oh those mortal hours of slow crawling
with jaded horses, the remaining miles; and when at last we
arrived my head was burning and I had cold shivers in every
limb; while there was the pale summer moon setting on the one
side, and the red summer sun rising on the other; so that as
usual I was between two fires, as I entered the little dirty mean
town of Hertford and drove up to the ' Dimsdale Arms.' Mrs.
C—— I told to give the boots of the inn a sovereign, to instantly
(it was then 5 o'clock a.m.), paste up my posters all over the town;
and he worked so zealously that before seven they *were* all over
the town.

Mrs. C—— persuaded me to go to bed for a few hours, I was
so ill; the doing so, and my bath, together, brought it to half-past
eleven, too late to go to the Mayor to ask for the use of the
Corn Exchange or Town Hall, or do anything but order a

brougham to drive to the hustings, where the speechifying and public virtue had already begun. And another provoking delay was Mrs. C—— making the discovery that she had blue ribbons in her bonnet, and stopping at a milliner's to change them for white, saying : " *Blue* is that infamous man's colour, and I won't wear it." As we drove into the field where the humbug was going on, the postillions of Sir LIAR's carriage, whom I did not know (as of course they were long since my time) stood up in their stirrups and took off their hats as I drove past. Around in front of the semi-circle of carriages before the hustings, I pulled the check and got out. For a moment I was in a perfect fever, for though I hope I shall never become that sponge of all iniquity, a human being without *moral* courage, I am fearfully afraid physically of a mob. But seeing their cowardly brute of a county member on the hustings before me, with that intensely, vulgar-looking personage, Lord and Lady PALMERSTON's bastard, the *soi-disant* Mr. W—— C—— for his bottle holder—so much for the political thimble-rig of the present day—I made one great effort over myself to do properly what I had come to do, and from a high fever that I was in the minute before, I became deadly cold and pale, and with it superhumanly calm and collected. So touching with my large green fan the arm of the first man near me, while Mrs. C—— followed closely holding my dress, I said in a loud clear voice, " My good people, make way for your member's wife, and let me pass, for I have something to say to him," whereupon the mob began to cheer and cry, " Make way for Lady L—— ; that we will, GOD bless her, poor lady." And instantly a clear passage was made for me up to the very scaffolding of the hustings. "Thank you, friends," said I. And then steadily fixing my eyes upon the cold, pale, fiendish, lack-lustre eyes of the electioneering baronet, I said, " Sir EDWARD EARLE BULWER L——, after turning me and my children out of our house to run an unexampled career of vice, you have spent years in promulgating every lie of me, and hunting me through the world with every species of persecution and outrage, your last gentlemanlike and manly attempt having been to try and starve me out : therefore, in return for your *lies*, I have come here to-day to say the *truths* I have to say of you, *to you*, openly and publicly. If you can deny *one* of the charges I shall bring against you, do so, but to *disprove* them I defy you."

Here, as the papers said, his jaw fell like that of a man suddenly struck with paralysis, and he made a rush from the hustings, valiantly trampling down the flower-beds of the house of Mr. STEPHEN AUSTIN, the editor of *The Hertford Mercury*, which was close at hand, by jumping over the pailings, and *heroically* locking himself into the dining-room. The moment the cowardly brute took to flight, the mob began to hiss and yell and vociferate, "Ah! he's guilty, he's guilty; he dare not face her. Three cheers for her ladyship." As soon as silence was restored, I turned to the crowd, who roared, "Silence, listen to what Lady L—— has to say." Whereupon I said, "Men of Herts, if you have the hearts of men, hear me." "We will, we will—speak up." Here a voice cried, "Stop, where is the *Times*' reporter?" to which several voices from the hustings cried out, "Oh, oh, he's been bundled off fast enough." Cries of "Shame." I then went on to tell them that their member's last conspiracy was to make out —because I dared to resent, having no brother to horsewhip him for his dastardly persecutions, and sending his infamous s'reet-walkers to insult me—that I was quite mad, in order to incarcerate me in a Madhouse. Cries of "Cowardly villain, but that won't do, after to-day, now that we have seen and heard you." I spoke for more than an hour. But I need not bore you with my speech, nor their plaudits, or the way in which they cheered and wanted to draw me back to the Hotel, which, thanking them cordially— I implored them not to do; as I had to go by the 3 o'clock train. Nor need I tell you how the roofs of the houses were covered with people, as well as the windows, waving handkerchiefs, and crying, "GOD bless you," when I went.

But this I will tell you, that, calling at the Mayor's before I went (for the people had asked me to address them in the Town Hall in the evening), as I wanted him to explain to them that I was tied to time and could not go; his wife told me that as I drove past to go to the hustings an old woman of 85, who lived in the village of Knebworth, and was a tenant of Sir LIAR's, and had been one of his grandfather's, and who came into Hertford occasionally to sell poultry, and who happened to be in the hall at the Mayor's house when I drove by, upon hearing it was I, and that I was going to the hustings, fell upon her knees and said, "Thank GOD! thank GOD! that I have lived to see this day, and that villain will be exposed at last, and poor dear Miss L——'s death avenged." I can only say that if the horrible opinion that *all* classes in the town of Hertford have of him be any criterion of that of those in the country (except that they, to be sure, belong to our putrescently rotten and profligate Aristocracy), it *is* a miracle how any amount of political jobbery or party bribery can get him returned.

Well, the journey back from Hertford being as hurried as the journey there, and I having been so ill when I set out, I was on my return, with all the painful excitement in addition, quite knocked up. And on the second day after my return, being in bed about 11 o'clock a.m., a card was brought to me with Mr. F—— H—— T——, 4, C—— Street, Piccadilly, on it, accompanied by a message that that gentleman wanted to see me particularly. "Why did you not say I was ill in bed, and could not see any one?" "HENRY told him so, my lady." "Then go and tell him so again." "The gentleman says he *must* see your ladyship, as it is for your advantage," was the answer to my message. "If he has any business, he can write," said I. "He can be no gentleman to persist in attempting to see a lady who is ill in bed, and a total stranger to him." Shortly after this I heard several voices loud in altercation outside my bedroom door, and Mrs. C——'s above them all, saying, "You shall *not* force your way in, unless you cut me down first." Whereupon I rang my bell, and Mrs. C—— came round the other way, through the drawing room, in a very excited state, and I said, "What on earth is the matter?" "A pack of wretches," said she, "evidently some of that villain Sir EDWARD's emissaries." "Let them in," said I, "and if they should attempt to carry me off bodily, send for the police. Now," added I, sitting up in bed, arranging the frills of my night things, and settling myself down to freezing point on the score of calmness and impassibility, as is my wont in every crisis that must be met, "unbolt the door, or rather unlock it" (for she had carried off the key that they should not force their way in during her absence), "and let them in." She did so; and in walked a little very dark man, with very black hair and eyes, of about 60, followed by a Patagonian woman of six feet high, who was a keeper from the Madhouse at Fairwater, near this, conducted by a Dr. W——. The giantess he told to sit down at one side of my bed, while he came round to the other, but followed by Mrs. C——. "Pray, Lady L——," said he, pulling out an election skit on blue paper, purporting to be Sir LIAR's address to his constituents, saying that one of the first measures he should propose in Parliament would be about "the social evil," to which he had always so largely contributed, and that as family ties and domestic duties had always been held so sacred by him, he regretted that his loved and honoured wife was not there to share his triumphs upon that occasion, as, although it might be considered a weakness in him, ambition had no charms for him but as it contributed to the happiness of his *alter ego* and those who blest his own fireside!!! and a great deal of similar *persiflage* and more pungent satire. Before I could reply, Mrs. C—— cried out, "No, I can answer for *that*, for I it was who, in great haste, got Lady L——'s placards printed—those on white paper pasted on the walls."

"No," said I, very quietly, "upon my honour I never saw that effusion before; but GOD bless the honest man who wrote it, whoever he be." "Your word is quite sufficient" said T——, who then, feeling my pulse the whole time—which he remarked was one of the most quiet and even he had ever felt—began divers florid panegyrics upon Sir LIAR's brilliant talents, success in life, and everything else that was exasperating, with the evident intention of exasperating me, in which he did *not* succeed. After an hour spent in this work, he went out of the room to consult with some one in another room, leaving the gaunt keeper in possession, and this round of going backwards and forwards he repeated till nine at night; for, of course, he had to earn the £100, which was his fee, for coming down here. Had I *then* known what Mrs. C—— told me after, *i.e.*, that the wretch L—— was the person in the other room, with whom he went to consult, and that there was a carriage with the horses to waiting *all* day at the other (Castle) Hotel, ready to carry me off to W——'s Madhouse, at Fairwater, I don't think I *could* have had sufficient control over myself to have retained my imperturbable calmness as I did.

When this T—— returned from a two hours' conference with the vile *Unknown* in the other room (during which time I had been very civil to the giantess, offering her luncheon), he again began feeling my pulse, and touching upon every irritating topic he could devise, and then upon European politics and other topics of the day; and then as a charming little variation he made me put out my tongue, looked at my teeth, and raised up my eyelids, in short, investigated me as minutely as if I had been a 500 guinea horse he was going to buy; after which, turning himself to the gaunt keeper, he said, "Well, I don't know. I think I never saw any one in sounder mind or body. What do *you* think?" "Why, really, sir," said the giantess, wiping her eyes, for which touch of human feeling I felt very grateful to her, "I *do* think *this* is one of the cruellest outrages I ever witnessed or heard of." "Humph," said T——, going out for another season of two hours' duration, which brought it to 5 o'clock before he returned, and when he did so, he was accompanied by Dr. W—— who pursued his plan of irritating topics, but with more provincial coarseness and vulgarity, culminating it all by saying in a sort of jibing way, "I must really say, Lady L——, that I think you are unreasonable to Sir EDWARD, for £400 a year is a very good allowance." "It might be for a mad Doctor or attorney's wife," I replied. "Ah! true—yes—a—certainly, that makes a difference." "And even then," added I, "they *might* be so *very* unreasonable as to want it *paid* in coin instead of *promissory* notes." Here ensued a series of telegrams of nods and winks between the two M.D.'s. So he again left the room, and I heard T—— mutter, "It won't do." When he returned again (without W——), it was 8 at night, so you may suppose what a day of *rest* I had after that horrid journey.

"Now, Lady L——," said T——, "I want you to oblige me by writing me a note, stating *what* terms you will accept from Sir EDWARD, to never again expose him as you did at Hertford on

Wednesday." " It's no use," said I, " it has been urged upon
him for years to give me a decent and punctual allowance; he
would rather part with his life than his money, and, moreover,
neither honour, nor oaths can bind him." "Well, but
what would you accept?" "Why, as one might as well
expect to get blood out of a stone as money out of him,
if I asked for an adequate income, I *know* he would never even
promise it; so if he will *really* give, that is, *pay* me £500 a-year
for *my* life; instead of a mythological £400 for his;—I'll not
again *publicly* expose him "—(were you here, I would *tell* you *how*
I came to be put off upon the original swindle of this disgraceful
£400 a-year; but it is too long to write). "Well, *do* write me a
note to that effect, and I'll go into your drawing-room while
you're writing it." "And what guarantee have *I*, pray Mr.
T——, that the gross outrage of to-day, so long hatching, shall
not be repeated?" " *My word of honour as a gentleman* (? ?)
Lady L——," said he, laying his hand upon his left side as he
walked into the drawing-room. "Do write the note," whispered
Mrs. C—— hurriedly,—" that man's your friend;—I'll tell you all
by-and-by." I shook my head and said, "I don't believe in
any *man's* friendship; more especially in a mad Doctor's, employed
by Sir EDWARD." When the note was finished, it was 9 o'clock!
I asked him when I should hear from him in reply to that note?
"In four days, at furthest," said he, as at length he rid me of
his presence. When he was gone, poor Mrs. C—— sank down
exhausted (as well she might be) into a chair. She then told me
the reason she had said he was my friend was, that L—— had
stormed, foamed, and stamped to *make* him and W—— sign a
certificate of my insanity. T—— said he *could* not; and
W—— he dare not. The latter moreover said, down in the Bar
—as he went away, "Mad! Lady L—— is no more mad than I
am; I'm afraid Sir EDWARD will find her only too sane."

I may as well tell you *here* before you have the pleasure of
meeting him again at his own house in Clarges-street, this H——
T——'s antecedents, which of course I did not learn until long
after. To begin with, he was a friend of L——'s, which com-
prises every other infamy,—and to show himself worthy of so
being, he had been dismissed from some Hospital, to which he
was surgeon. Not only the stipulated four days, but nine, had
elapsed, without my hearing from Mr. T—— the result of the
note he had made me write. I then wrote to him to enquire the
reason of this? His reply did not even allude to the subject,
but was a rigmarole about the weather; as if he had been writing
to an idiot, who did not require a rational answer to any question they had asked. So I again wrote to say—that having been
so grossly outraged I was not going to be insulted and fooled by
him, and that if he did not send me a definite and explicit reply

to the note I had written at his urgent request before the following Tuesday, or the following Wednesday, I should call at his house, and according to the answer I then received, should know how to act. Now my plan was, that in case of again being fooled by these wretches, to take two of Sir LIAR's infamous letters with me, which he has denied upon oath ; the one, a threat before the publication of my first book, saying, " *he would ruin me if I published that, or any other book* "—the other a letter he had written me after one of his tigerish onslaughts, in which he had frightfully bitten my cheek, in which he says, " You have been to me perfection as a wife, I have eternally disgraced myself, I shall go abroad, change a name which is odious to me,—take £200 a year, and leave you all the rest." Fancy that selfish, pompous Sybarite, profligate brute, on £200 a year ! But saying is *one* thing and doing another, as his friend DIZZY and my Lord DERBY know. By these letters I was determined to seek the only redress left to me that could not in the *onset* be tampered with, that of a common woman ; by going to a London Police office, letting the Magistrate read them, and stating my Lord DERBY's *creditable* Colonial Secretary's recent persecutions, which statement he could not prevent being taken down by the reporters, and appearing in all the next day's papers. This was my plan, in case that loathsome ruffian, Sir L——, was insane enough not to accede to the ridiculously moderate and lenient terms I had offered him, after his life-long, dastardly, and fiendish rascality. Well, on the Tuesday evening, having heard nothing further from T——, Mrs. CLARK and I set off for London. With my usual good fortune, the Great Western, and all the neighbouring Hotels, were full, and we could only get rooms at a horrid dirty hole, opposite the Marble-arch, where we arrived at 8 in the morning. After washing, dressing, and breakfasting, we set off for C—— street, getting out at the corner of Piccadilly, and telling the brougham to wait there ; and as St. James's clock was striking 12 on Wednesday, 22nd of June, 1858—for GOD knows I never can forget the day !—I knocked at Mr. II—— T——'s door. We were shown up into the drawing-room. Presently the fellow came to us —holding out *both* his hands (which, of course, I did not see, but retained mine to hold my parasol ;) saying he was delighted to see me (no doubt), and hoped I was come to dine with him !!! " Mr. T——," said I, " I have neither come to dine with you nor to be fooled by you. I come to know what you have done with that note, which you so entreated me to write, proposing terms to Sir EDWARD L——." " That note ! that note !—let me see," said he, tapping his forehead, as if he had to go back into the night of ages to find out *what* note I alluded to. And after this piece of by-play—he said, suddenly, " Oh ! oh ! that note you wrote at Taunton. I gave it to L——." I now knew what to expect. But you had better, in his interest, communicate with Sir EDWARD L——, and tell him I *must* have a definite answer one way or the other, for which 1 shall call at six o'clock this evening. Good morning." I then went to call upon Miss R——; and she asked to come with me, to be present when I returned to T——'s; and fortunately 1 gave her Sir LIAR'S two infamous letters to take care of, lest I, in my agitation, should drop or mislay them. At six, she, Mrs. CLARKE, and I, again drove to the corner of C—— street, and there got out. As we did so, I observed an impudent-looking, snub-nosed man, who was walking up and down, and stared at me in the most impudent and determined manner, as if he had been watching for us, as afterwards turned out to be the case. We were again shown up into the drawing-room at T——'s, but *this* time the folding-doors were closed between the two rooms, and we heard the murmuring of low voices in the back room. After being kept waiting more than half an hour, I rang the bell, and told the servant to say, "That if I could not see Mr. T——, I must go." The wretch then soon after made his appearance, saying he had been detained by patients; and soon after him stalked into the room a tall, raw-boned, hay-coloured-hair Scotchman, who I subsequently learned was an apothecary of the name of R——, keeping a druggist's shop in Fenchurch-street (another friend of L——'s, of course, and the second with T——, who signed the certificate of my insanity!—he never having seen me, or 1 him before, and I never having *once* spoken to him!). This fellow, like all the other employees, began talking of—quite *a propos de bottes* —Sir LIAR'S extraordinary cleverness! Whereupon, Miss R——, in a passion, took his cheek-biting letter out of her pocket, and read it to him, adding, "Perhaps you think this brutality another proof of his cleverness?" "Evidently a man of great sensibility!!" said the lean apothecary when she had finished. I could not stand this, and finding I was to get no answer about the letter from T——, I said to Miss R—— and Mrs. CLARKE, "Come, don't let us waste any more time in being fooled and insulted here, we'll go." Easier said than done, for upon reaching the hall we found it literally filled with two mad Doctors, that fellow, his assistant, the impudent snub-nosed man who had stared so when I got out of the brougham —two women keepers, one a great Flanders mare of six feet high, the other a moderate-sized, and nice-looking woman, and a very idiotic-looking footman of T——'s, with his head against the hall door, to bar egress, and who seemed to have acquired as an *amateur* that horrible Mad Doctor's trick of rolling his head and never looking *at* any one, but over *their* heads, as if he saw some strange phantasmagoria in the air above them; and which that fellow had to such a degree, that I am *certain* any nervous or

weak-minded person would, from sheer physical irritation, have
been driven mad *really* in a very short time ; and no doubt that
is what it is done for. Seeing this blockade, I exclaimed, "What
a set of blackguards ; " to which Mr. H——, wagging his head,
and phantom-hunting over mine, with his pale, poached egg-un-
speculative eyes—said, " I beg you'll speak like a lady—Lady
L——." " I am treated so like one, that I certainly ought," I
replied. Hearing a loud talking in the dining-room, into which
Mrs. C—— had been summoned by T——, I walked into it, in
time to hear her very energetically saying, "I wont," to some
proposition they were making to her, and seeing a side door
that led into a back room again, I looked in, and there saw that precious brace of scoundrels, Sir LIAR, COWARD, SWINDLER himself,
and " that sublime of rascals, his Attorney—listening! for the
dastardly brute always fights shy," with his vizor down, from
behind an ambush ; but from the stabs in the back, and the force
of the blows, there is no mistaking one's antagonists. So, boldly ad-
vancing towards him, " You cowardly villain," said I, " this is the
second time I have confronted you this month ; *why* do you always
do your dirty work by deputy, except when you used to leave the
marks of your horse teeth in my flesh ; and boldly strike a defenceless woman." At this, the reptile rushed, as he had done at the
Hertford hustings, but this time not into Mr. AUSTIN's flower gar-
den, but down Mr. H—— T——'s kitchen stairs ! and up his area
steps ! into the open street. I turned to Miss R——, who had followed me, and said, " See, the contemptible wretch has taken to
his heels." Whereupon, going into the hall, she pushed the idiotic
footman aside and said, " Whatever villainy you are paid to
practise towards Lady L——, you have no *right* to detain *me*."
T—— ordered the hall door to be unchained and unlocked, and
she rushed out into the street. Talk of novels ! She told me
after, that at the corner of Piccadilly, she stumbled up against a
young man, and said—" Oh sir, for GOD's sake, get me a cab,
they are taking in the most iniquitous manner a friend of mine
to an asylum, the best friend I ever had, to whom I owe everything, Lady L——, and she is no more mad than you are." The
young man turned deadly pale, staggered against the wall, and
said in a voice scarcely audible, " I am very sorry I can't
interfere."—The young man was my own wretched son !
   Meanwhile I, who was again sitting in T——'s hall—said,
" Nothing shall get me out of this." Whereupon the hall door
was opened, and two policemen were brought in, at which I
started to my feet, and said, " Don't presume to touch me, I'll
go with these vile men, but the very stones of London shall rise
up against them, and their infamous employers." " That shall
they," said Mrs. CLARKE, " they'll get the worst of it." She told
me after, that when she had told T—— and L——, in the dining

room, that a stirring investigation would be made which would be their ruin, instructed by their infamous employer, they had quite laughed in her face, and said, "Pooh! nonsense, Lady L—— has lived out of the world so long, she has *no* friends, and there can be no investigation made, and Sir EDWARD is at the top of the tree." "Well, before you are much older, you will see whether she has friends or not, and whether this villainy will pass off with impunity," she replied. At the advent of the policemen, I got into H——'s carriage, which was in waiting. He, the *two* keepers, Mrs. CLARKE, and myself inside, and the impudent-looking, snub-nosed assistant on the box. The wretches took me all through the Park, and as there had been a breakfast at Chiswick that day, it was crowded; many whom I knew kissed their hands in great surprise to see me. Ah! thought I, you little know *where* they are dragging me to! Arrived at Mr. H——'s stronghold, a very fine house in fine grounds, which had formerly belonged to the Duke of CUMBERLAND (and which *since* my incarceration H—— has been obliged to leave, and transfer himself to London, public indignation having made it too hot for him), as Mrs. CLARKE knew nothing of London, fortunately I had the presence of mind to ask the name and *locale* of my prison, and write it down upon one of my cards for her, that she might bring me my things from the hotel. I was then shown upstairs, after she left me, into a large bedroom, with the *two* keepers, and the windows duly *nailed* down, and only opening about three inches from the top. After kneeling down and praying to GOD in a perfect agony, I bathed my face in cold water, and the little keeper was very kind and feeling, and said to me, "Oh pray, my lady, try and keep calm under this severe trial; it does seem to me to be something very monstrous, and depend upon it, GOD will never let it go on." "I know He will not," said I, and then looking out at the window, or rather through it, I saw between 30 and 40 women walking in the grounds. "Are all these unfortunates incarcerated here?" I asked of the little keeper. "Those," said she, rather evasively, "are our ladies; they are out gathering strawberries." I then rang the bell, and when it was answered, I said, "I want to see Mr. H——." He came, and before I could speak, said, "It's a lovely evening. You had better come out and take a walk, Lady L——." "Mr. H——," said I, "I sent for you to *order* you to remove those two keepers from my room, for I am *not* mad *as you* very well know, and I won't be driven mad by being treated as a maniac, and as for walking out, or associating with those poor creatures out there, if they really are insane, I'll not do it, if I am kept in your Mad-house for 10 years." "Mad-house, mad-house, nonsense! Lady L——, this is no mad-house, and those are my children." " Then you must be a perfect DANAUS," said I, "for there are about 50 of them. But if you had a hundred, I again *order* you to remove these women from my room, and at your peril disobey me." He then told them to leave the room, and went himself soon after. In about half-an-hour I heard my door unlocked on the outside, and a gentle knock at the door; I said, "Come in," and a charming little girl of about 14, with a pretty gentle expression of face, soft chestnut hair, and the prettiest and almost dove-like dark hazel eyes I ever saw, came in with some tea and some strawberries. This was H——'s eldest daughter, and how he and his odious vulgar wife came by such a child, I can't imagine, unless the fairies stole theirs, and left this one in exchange. This dear little girl, my only conso-lation while there, conceived a most violent affection for me, which I heartily returned, for she was a perfect star in the desert, and with a big fat magnificent tortoiseshell cat, with the most fascinating manners, a perfect feline CHESTERFIELD! and the poor cow, which that brute H—— used to leave in an arid field, under a vertical sun, without water (the pump being *deranged*, like his patients), were my only comforts; and as I and poor little MARY H—— used to pump for hours at this crazy pump, till we filled the stone trough for the poor cow, which used to bound and caper like a dog, when it saw us coming to the rescue; *this* was no doubt considered as a strong proof of my insanity; or at least of my having *water* on my brain! I never *would* go into the grounds with my keepers, only with my dear, gentle, affectionate little MARY. And moreover Mr. H—— sent *all* his " children " to his other Madhouse farther on the road, so that I had the Palladian Villa all to myself, without even the three kings. The first evening poor Mrs. CLARKE returned about 10 o'clock with my scanty wardrobe. I *implored* her *not*, by way of consulting a lawyer, to go to Mr. H——, who after the LYNDHURST papers and SELLER's affair, I believed to be the thorough rascal he eventually proved himself to be. But unfortunately, at Miss R——'s instigation, she *did;* for your friends (?) always know your affairs better than you do yourself. It appeared that two days after I was incarcerated in Mr. H——'s stronghold, and Mrs. CLARKE had returned to Taunton to rouse up the people, which she did to good purpose! that ruffian L—— came down here, and brought with him a solicitor, a Mr. E—— B——, saying he had come for my tin boxes and all my papers! "Then," said Mrs. CLARKE, "you won't have one of them." Of course, the provincial attorney thought the great man, and that sacred Mumbo Jumbo of a husband! (no matter how infamous) ought to be omnipotent, and that she should give them up. But she would not; and some commercial traveller in the hotel, hearing the altercation between them, very kindly called her out of the room, and said, "Ask him to show you his warrant, or authority for making such a demand. And if the fellow won't or can't, then I'll know how to deal with him." She did so, and the wretch said he had his order in his pocket. "Well then, produce it," said the traveller, coming in, "and if you won't I'll send for a constable to turn you out of this." At which the attorney said, in all humble sycophancy, to L——, "My dear sir, you had better produce your authority." But as the wretch, of course, could not produce what he had not got, he was bundled out neck and crop by the commercial traveller. But as he went, he turned to Mrs. CLARKE, clenching his fist, and said, "Take my word for it, you will never see Lady L—— again, nor will anyone else." "And take my word for it, Mr. L——, that this threat of yours will turn out as great a falsehood as everything else you have ever said," was her answer. This it was, I suppose, made my friend feel I should be made away with in the Madhouse; in which, though no doubt Sir LIAR's intention, like most utterly unscrupulous villains, he had overreached himself, for as Mr. H—— was to get £1,000 a year for keeping me there, it is not likely to oblige his patron he'd have jeopardized his neck by poisoning me. L—— when going, as a *pis aller*, turned round and said, "Ah! by-the-by, Mrs. CLARKE, Sir EDWARD wants to see you, to pay you your bill." She said, "I'd rather forfeit every shilling of my bill, than stay one instant in the room with such a villain. He need not fear, I'll take care to have my bill paid, and no thanks to him."

At H——'s the rule of the house was about two inches of candle to go to bed with, for fear of some mad incendiary, and then the door double locked upon you outside, but as I was *not* either mad or an incendiary, and am in the habit of making my ablutions, and reading, and saying my prayers before I go to bed, I could not do with the two inches, and so effectually resisted the candle rule, but could do nothing against the locked door, and therefore was greatly frightened the next morning, for the first time one awakens in a strange place one cannot for a few seconds remember where one is; so I was frightened at seeing the great Flanders mare keeper standing over me, who said, "I came to call you, but your ladyship seemed in such a happy sleep, I did not like to wake you." I told H—— that this must not happen again, but she must wait till I rang. He then said he meant to get me a *maid* the next day, which was a delicate way of putting it, considering that the Flanders mare's successor was even more strapping, only dark, and the image, or rather the *facsimile*, of "The Fair SOPHIA" in CRUIKSHANK'S Ballad of "Lord BATEMAN," if she had only worn a turban instead of a cap, and had had a gold warming-pan of a watch at her side. Her name was SPARROW, but she never was

in the way when I wanted her, her excuse being, the house
had a flat Italian roof, and she used to sit out there to work, the
"*prospec*" was so rural! "But SPARROW," said I, "you were
got to attend upon me, and so should not, like the rest of your
species, sit alone upon the house-top." Everything was so
atrociously bad in this fine house that I really could not eat, and
I believe H—— began to fear that I should die upon his hands,
so at the end of four or five days he said to me, " What can I
get you? What do you have for breakfast at Taunton?"
" What I am not likely to get here, Mr. H——, an appetite."
But what I really suffered most from in that intensely hot summer, being a water-drinker, and the water here being the finest
I ever tasted in any part of the world, was the horrible tepid
ditchwater at H——'s ; and when I tried the soda water, that
was equally bad. 1 was also thoroughly wretched without my
clothes and books or a single thing I was accustomed to. H——,
it is true, was *very* anxious to send for *all* my goods and chattels
to Taunton, which you may be *quite sure* I would not let him do ;
as I told him it was not worth while for the very short time I
was sure public indignation would allow me to remain incarcerated in his stronghold. One day Mrs. H——, a thoroughly
vulgar, selfish, inane "British *female*," as they very properly and
zoologicaly call themselves, and who moulted her h's in reckless
profusion, came and informed me that Mr. H—— was gone to
*H*ascot, and would I like to take a drive with her? I said,
" Yes, I should be very glad indeed to breathe a little fresh
air," for, like herself, Mr. H—— had made me *Ill*, too, by that
eternal phantasmagoria wagging of his head, and rolling of his
eyes. After having *faits mes premières amies* with madame, oh! joy,
little MARY and I were sent out to drive alone, so that I really
might have made my escape with ease, only I had given my word I
would not. When I had been there about ten days, those
patent humbugs the Commissioners made their visit. They were
Dr. H—— and that vile old Dr. C——, who as Dr. OILY GAMMON
ROBERTS said, would sell his own mother, or do anything else
for money; but there to be sure comes in the literary elements
again, for has he not published some rubbish about ' Hamlet '?
and so it is throughout, even the cheap and nasty *Daily Telegraph*, or Court plaister, as it is now called, which began not only
by lapidating and crucifying Sir LIAR, but also by spatchcock-
ing him, on the top of a *column*, like saint somebody, one of the
early martyrs before martyrdom became a civilized institution.
The moment Mr. DICKENS'S chum, the literary scamp and *de-
bauchee*, Mr. S——, is enrolled on its staff—*il fait volte face*, and
began puffing him in the most batefaced and outrageous manner.
The other Commissioner was Mr. PROCTOR—BARRY CORNWALL, by
far the best, and most gentlemanlike of them—and who listened

to my statement with marked attention, saying with a shrug of the shoulders, "Those letters I confess startled me." The letters he alluded to were two I had written to Sir LIAR touching some of his infamies, for there is no vice that he has left unexhausted, and no virtue unassumed. But as I told Mr. PROCTOR, the charges in those letters were no inventions of mine, and I gave him my authority, which was that when I was at Geneva, my old friend, the *Comtesse Marie de Warenzon*, came to me one morning and said she had got a letter from her niece, Lady PEMBROKE, and she must read me one paragraph—"That disgusting wretch Sir E—— B—— L—— has just been drummed out of Nice—*not* Vice—for his infamy with *women*." Before these Commissioners I turned to that great walrus H——, who stood like a footman at a respectful distance in their presence, and I said, " Now Mr. H——, I have been nearly a fortnight in your house, can you say from your conscience—if you have one?— that I have said, done, or looked any one thing that could in any way make you think I was not in the full and clear, and very analytic possession of my intellect ? " H—— wagged his head, twirled his thumbs, and rolled his poached egg orbs fearfully, phantom-hunting, as he mumbled in a low voice " I'd rather not give an opinion." " Of course not," said I, " having taken the ghost's word for a thousand pounds yearly ! But pray, if you believe me in any even the slightest degree insane, how can you reconcile it to your conventionality towards these gentlemen the Commissioners, to leave your very charming little daughter unguarded with me all day long, and worse still, allow her to drive with me alone ! when from one minute to another, I might do her some grievous bodily harm, or make my escape with ease." At this, without wasting a reply on me, Mr. H——, began sonorously clearing some imaginary obstruction in his throat, and reminded the Commissioners that they would be late for the train. I may as well tell you here, what of course I only heard from her and others after, *i.e.*, that Miss RYVES it was, after rushing out of T——'s house, and nearly stumbling over Mr. L——, who drew up, and sent to the papers a true and circumstantial account of my most iniquitous kidnapping and incarcerations, which the infamous time-serving *Times*, of course, did not insert ; she also wrote to the Hertford papers, to say she had been for years witness to, and cognisant of Sir EDWARD'S persecutions of me, and my maid was (and thank GOD *is*) still living, who had been witness to his personal brutalities in former times, and in short, that out of Hell there was not such an iniquitous pair as my Lord DERBY'S Colonial Secretary, and his Attorney L——. Now *pray bear these facts well in mind.* I may also as well here mention a circumstance touching Miss RYVES, which from its absurd triviality I should have indubitably have forgotten, but for the infamous lie that unscrupulous ruffian, Sir EDWARD, founded upon it, in converting this parasite into a relation!!!! of mine with whom I had gone abroad by my own choice!!—The circumstance to which I allude, is this. My father's maternal grandfather, Lord MASSEY, was godfather to Miss RYVES'S father! whereupon she and her brothers (now, poor young men, both dead) called themselves MASSEY RYVES; but I really don't think that even in Ireland, that land of cousins, the most distant relationship could be fabricated out of that! otherwise, I am related to the GRATTANS, as the great GRATTAN was my mother's godfather, and very fond of her. But England being the land of *cozening*, that King of Cozeners and Swindlers, Sir EDWARD ——, actually had the effrontery to forge a relationship between me and his tool, to suit his own ever nefarious purposes. What matter who detected and laughed at the cheat? Lord MELBOURNE used to say that "if a lie lived only *half an hour*, it would do its work," and upon this plan has Sir LIAR acted all his life, which, I suppose, is what he would call "*Half hours with the best Authors*," to wit, the Devil and himself. The Sunday after the humbug visit of the Commissioners, an oppressively hot day, the door was unlocked, and Mr. HYDE tottered into my room, for he was then suffering from softening of the brain (but certainly not of the heart), the complaint of which he afterwards died. His hands were full of papers, and he said, in his bluff, bull-dog way, "Well! I've seen Sir EDWARD in Downing-street." "Dear me," said I, "you seem quite overpowered with the honour!" "I saw him yesterday," said he, "and though it's almost too bad to show you, yet you must see it; I mean the statement he and L—— drew up for the Commissioners respecting your insanity."

This precious piece of documentary rascality set forth that both my father and mother died mad——Now my father had had one of the most absurdly splendid public funerals for a Commoner that ever was seen, being Grand Master of some Masonic Lodge —and ostentatious burials are not generally bestowed on lunatics; and my poor mother having been only ten years dead, anyone could have refuted *that* lie. But like all the villainous lies, they were only fabricated for the *few*, and for the *dark*, and never allowed to appear in the honest searching light of publicity. This tissue of lies went on to say that I had attempted to commit suicide!! and that the family insanity in me had developed itself in *delirium tremens!!!!* from my intemperate habits!!!!!! "The dastardly fiend!" I exclaimed, "so the sacrilegious monster would even desecrate my poor mother's and father's graves! for what? to bury his life-long victim alive in a Madhouse. It is true, but worse, far worse than that, this unscrupulous demon would, without one touch of remorse, brand with a triple hereditary taint of insanity his only son! at least his only legitimate son, who will have the quite sufficient misfortune of inheriting the name of so infamous a father." "Yes—'pon my soul it's too bad," said the Attorney, "but I'm happy to tell you that I have now got you the £500 a-year for *your* life." I knew by this, though all papers but the conveniently reticent *Times* had been kept from me, that the public indignation must be astir, and making things rather unpleasant for my Lord DERBY'S creditable Colonial Secretary, in which I was right, for I afterwards heard that not only the people here were holding committees and meetings every day on the outrage of which I had been the victim; and the Somersetshire Yeomanry were determined upon going mounted to London, and pulling his house about his ears if I were not released; but that his Butler could literally scarcely stand under the loads of letters he had to bring in every morning of imprecations and threats, by no means *anonymous*, and as poor Prince ALBERT was then living (for our little selfish, sensuous, inane and carnal Queen would not care if all her subjects were equally distributed in Madhouses, or pounded in mortars), my Lord DERBY was sent for in hot haste by her Majesty, and told, either I must be instantly set at liberty or his Colonial Secretary must resign; for the outrage, or rather the scandal, was too great; for *that's* the only thing they dread, being quite of TARTUFFE'S opinion *que pecher en secret n'est pas pecher, ce ne que l'eclat qui fait le crime.* Now, my woman's intuition and common sense told me that something of this sort must be going on, or I should never have heard a syllable of the £500 for my life. So in reply to Mr. HYDE'S *obliging communication*, I said; "What! are they trying to make me out an idiot as well as a maniac, that they, or you, should suppose after such an irreparable culminating outrage as he has inflicted upon me by this incarceration, I will let that scoundrel Sir EDWARD off on the beggarly pittance I would have accepted before it? and oblige him by vegetating upon it in the exile of some living tomb, for the rest of the life he has so poisoned at every source. No thank you." "Well," said the Attorney, who had at that time received his bribe, to say nothing of breathing the air of Downing-street, and being brought into *personal* contact with the Magnates of THE PARTY, which would do to brag among the snobocracy of Ely-place, Highgate, and Langport for the rest of his life. "Well," said he, "Sir EDWARD has shown me his rental, and how he is tied up, and he really cannot"—"Pray Mr. HYDE," said I, interrupting him; "*are* you Sir EDWARD'S solicitor or mine?" Whereupon, not finding it convenient or agreeable to endure any probing, he scrambled up all his papers, and said, taking out his watch—"Bless me, I shall lose the train," and darted off out of the room.

ROSINA, LADY LYTTON.

The next day, Dr. OILY GAMMON ROBERTS, whom I had known a long time, called upon me. He had just had the supreme felicity of becoming Lord PALMERSTON'S medical attendant, and is just the smooth, mellifluous, double-dealing, Jesuitical personage, who would be happy to accept a reversionary emetic from any of the peers or peeresses whom he attends, (or) though an infidel, to do any amount of canting with Lord SHAFTESBURY in Exeter Hall in the morning, or any amount of pimping for Lady SHAFTESBURY all the evening. The dear Conservatives having fallen upon evil days, *via* their Colonial Secretary, was of course nuts to the dear Whigs, though as far as any amount of dirty work, back-stair climbing, and athletic, indefatigable, political, and every other sort of jobbery, the two parties are in reality "*one* concern;" and having the same "bonnets," during their alternate ins and outs, always know the exact thimble the pea lurks under. Well, Dr. OILY GAMMON came, and his manner was a perfect emulsion of almonds when I told him of Mr. HYDE'S audacious proposition about the £500 a year. He urged me to be firm and not take a doit less than a thousand a year; which, as he truly said, was little enough after such an outrage. "For which," said I, "no money could compensate." "Very true," said he, and after assuring me of the universal indignation and sympathy my case had excited; he took his departure, promising soon to call again. The plot was now evidently thickening, for the next morning the fair SOPHIA, alias SPARROW, came twittering into my room, and said a groom had ridden out in such haste that the horse was covered with foam to tell Mr. H. he must go to London without a *moment's* delay; and "I cannot but think and hope," said she, "that it means some good to your ladyship." About five o'clock H. returned from town, more fat, frowsy, head-wagging, and eye-rolling, than ever; but desperately civil! and *aux petits soins*, and asked me if I would like a drive as far as Richmond? I said, "Yes, amazingly, provided Miss H. went with us." "Oh yes, certainly," said he, with a smile, or rather a dyspeptic leer, which he meant to be half *prevenant*, half paternal, but which only made him look as

"Hyenas in love are supposed for to look, or
A something between ABELARD and old BLUCHER."

"Oh, certainly, for your ladyship has quite bewitched my little MARY, and she cries every time a servant is sent up to you with anything instead of her." Never was anything so beautiful! as that always lovely view from Richmond Hill upon that glorious July evening, with the golden sun steeping it in light and turning the "Silver Thames" into a perfect Pactolus, while the fresh breeze from the river was a real luxury after my nearly three weeks' incarceration in that large, but low-ceilinged stuffy room, with its nailed down windows. And as caged birds are always wild when they do get out, MARY HILL and I took to running races, and not the least part of the pleasure of which to me was seeing old fat H—— "Like panting Time, toiling after us in vain," and puffing and blowing like a steam engine; till he made almost as much noise as all his ten children with their hoops and skipping ropes under my windows of a morning, when, groaning in my cage, I used to say, " Why skip ye so ye little HILLS?"

By the time we got back to T—— L—— the evening was fast closing in, and though as always I had an invitation to sit below in a really magnificent groined lofty roofed banquetting room, some 50 feet long, that they had there, I always preferred my own society, even with my own ills, to Mrs. H—— and all her Ills,—which with the greatest Ill of all—her husband—made a party of thirteen of them, which yet did not comprise *all* the ills that flesh is heir to.

And now comes the most horrible and cruel part of this history, and which is so painful to me to write, or rather to excavate out of the desolate grave of all my hopes, where it has lain buried for the last five years and a half, and where I thought it would remain till GOD had mercy on me and I was buried with it. But it would have been impossible to tell you all the rest without telling this too; or you would really think me not only mad, but a liar, that I had not in our Courts of Justice, or more frequently of Injustice, fully exposed, and got at least as much redress as public indignation and condemnation can afford to the Victim, when bestowed upon the perpetrators of such dastardly and chronic and complex infamy. But Sir EDWARD does not do his fiendish work by halves. He knew that from me *he* could never expect mercy nor longer forbearance. So he, with demoniacal and *unscrupulous* astuteness baited the trap with the two lacerated hearts of both Mother and Child; for he knew that even to expose him I would not, and could not, expose my own son—whom GOD forgive—though I firmly believe that *he*, at *first*, was as much duped as I was. For though under ordinary circumstances—he was well aware, from bitter experience, that he could not believe in any promise his father ever made—still he naturally thought that after standing upon the brink of such a ruinous Abyss, and having been only saved by nature's great miracle, a Mother's Love—he would for once in fear and trembling have kept faith with his victims wholly and solely in his own sordid and selfish interest. And so this truly unhappy young martyr did evil that good might come of it; and that, as he at the time told me, he might buy his Mother back at any price. It is WALTER SCOTT, I think, who says— " There can be no Virtue without Truth, and there can be no

Truth without Moral Courage." But where was this poor predestined young victim to acquire that? when the whole course of his accursed literary training was to *develope* his intellect, and *stultify* his moral qualities, by, from his youth denying to his *naturally* gentle and affectionate nature the holy vigils of a Mother's care, and the humanizing and heart-expanding influences of HOME. While the diplomatic obligations of his detestable profession could not fail to weaken to annihilation that plebeian appendage called conscience; so surely does custom blunt and familiarize either the worst or most frightful things. No wonder then that I should have no admiration for, but a positive contempt for, mere intellect; as intellect without a moral *fulcrum* is, of all the Devil's levers, the one that raises the most fearful preponderances of evil, and causes them to float buoyantly and triumphantly over the world. But I must get on, and get over this last heartquake of mine as rapidly as I can. GOD knows I would not injure him in the world's estimation (little as it is worth) more than he has already injured himself; and GOD, I am convinced, has punished him far more than He has thought fit to afflict me. Five years and a half since this crowning iniquity have I waited, hoping against hope that now, that he was no longer a Boy, he would shake off the glamour of his father's terrorism, and show some spark of manliness and human feeling, if only as a sort of expiatory conscience tax to GOD. But when was conscience, courage, or feeling, ever evinced by either a B—— or a L——? For the rest of this disgraceful history, I should be only too glad if you proclaimed it at the market cross. But *that* I am very sure you will not do; as I am fully aware of the requirements of literary amenities and social conventionalities; and therefore it is that I have lived too long alone with GOD, and the bitter sorrows He has sent me, not to gauge everything by simple Truth, unalloyed by expediency; and, perhaps too, as ESMOND says, " I have seen too much of success in life to take off my hat and huzza to it, in its gilt coach, as it passes." I am also fully aware of literary posthumous chivalry, and its Bayard courage! upon the safe vantage ground of posterity! therefore, when I have been dead some hundred years,—how pens will start from their inkstands, like swords from their scabbards, to avenge me! while Electric Caligraphy will not have left sufficient ink in Christendom to blacken Sir EDWARD, the CÆSAR BORGIA of the nineteenth century (with the beauty and the courage left out) up to his natural hue. Gentlemen of 1964, I cannot find words to thank you—for all I shall have to say then, is what I pray now—*Implora Pace!*

Well, on the evening after my return from Richmond, while I was at tea, the door was thrown open and Miss R—— was announced. I reproached myself with ingratitude at the time, but she was more antipathetic to me than ever; her manner was so brusque, coarse, and unfeeling—meeting me for the first time in such a place. And she did look so dreadfully ugly, and so additionally dirty! a great *tour de force!* that I recoiled from her touch, and when she said, without any preparation in that sharp, shrill, cracked bell of a voice of hers, "Shure I've brought *your* son to see you," I felt almost as though she had knocked me down, and burst out crying—"Then," said I, "I won't see him; he has never acted like a son to me; and I suppose his infamous father is springed in his own trap, and he has sent his son to get him out of it." For two hours ineffectually, for I would not yield to this evident bullying, did Miss R——, with her usual want of tact, want of feeling, and coarse uncouthness, irritate every nerve in my body. I may as well here give you the keynote of her character. It is an inane and egregious vanity—and a mania *pour se faire personnage;* one of that dangerous class of meddling fools, who are for ever rushing in "where angels fear to tread." She was indeed "a thing of shreds and patches," made up of the fragments of other person's thoughts and opinions—which she invariably retailed as her *own.* In all things a mere ape and echo. During the Crimean War, she read up the leaders in the *Times,* and Mr. RUSSELL's letters, and then thought herself quite competent to argue with, or rather to dictate to the first military authorities, past, or present. Vilely ill-educated, or rather not educated at all, she could not open her mouth without mutilating the QUEEN's English, and, like "The Wife of Bath," her "French was French of Bow," or, rather, of Bœotia—"for French of Paris knew she none," and her grotesque and barbaric pronunciation of what she called such, was worthy of Sir EDWARD himself! or of that other universal genius (in his own opinion) Mr. W—— R——. She also had, like most vain fools, a literary mania, and a great ambition to appear very *blue.* I am confident, from her subsequent ingratitude towards me, who, as she acknowledged to my son, was the only benefactress she had ever had, that next to her fear, by my incarceration for life, of losing an excellent milch cow, which she had no chance of replacing, her motive in writing to the papers, and making my iniquitous abduction public, was that she thought by so doing she should put herself forward, and become quite a heroine. I am also certain that when Sir LIAR got hold of her, and that other patent scoundred E—— J—— (who had been plied for him by that little Red Rat, COCKBURN—as of course it does not do for a Chief Justice to *appear* in dirty work, all English virtue, being strictly PUBLIC!), seeing the empty, heartless, vain, unprincipled ass they had to deal with, they fooled her to the very top of her bent; the rascally Q.C. telling her, that he, Sir

LIAR'S *ame damnée*, had only undertaken the business in *my* and my son's interest; and what a thing it would be for her to heal family differences! and what a proud position for her, a young girl (39), to be the sole pivot that could keep the DERBY Ministry in! and E—— J——, knowing that there was no friend like a woman, and no head like a woman's, when dictated to by her heart. All this I learned from herself after; but where it struck me, like an electric flash, how they had fooled, and sold—or rather *bought*—her, for I was the sold! was her saying, the day I left H——'s stronghold, and we were driving to town, as she pointed out of the window to the Asylum for Idiots, on the left-hand side of the road, and said, with one of her vain-glorious chuckles, " As E—— J—— said, ' we won't put *you* there, Miss R——!'" "Then," said I, " I am certain that he, and his infamous client, *must* have fooled you to their heart's content." I have no doubt, too, that when she heard the jingle of the thimbles, about keeping the DERBY Ministry in! and she being the sole pivot! that could secure the Cabinet!! a vista opened to her of all the salons in London; *ibid*, the becoming an honorary member of all the literary cliques; and ditto, of her being made free of the sesame of all the backstairs in Downing-street! To say nothing of her having fallen desperately in love with Mr. L——! (poor fellow, how soon his punishment over-took him), whom she used to rave about as the *bo*-eye-dale (alias *beau ideal*) of what a young poet ought to be; so handsome, so elegant, so charming! and I have no doubt in the plenitude of her imbecile conceit, she thought she would fasten herself on me, as a daughter-in-law, for the rest of my life. What a pity she could not hear the loathing disgust that her *bo-eye-dale* used to speak of her with. At all events, it is some comfort to know how those he-villains—the brand new Baronet, and the outlawed, swindling Q.C.—squeezed the orange and then threw away the rind, and when they had got all they wanted of her, kicked her off in a way *quite* worthy of them. And it is also a consolation, that, as a Frenchman said to me, when she used to be talking about her *cost hume de cheval* (Amazone), as she called her habit, "*Ah! madame, quel bonheur puisque que cette drolesse la c'en est amourachée de monsieur votre fils qu'elle ne peut jamais devenir votre belle-fille!*"

And now, before telling you what remains of this terrible history I must exonerate my unhappy Son from ever having gone such lengths in impious falsehood and hypocrisy, as to have written that disgusting "Dedication of Lucile" to his infamous father's "loved" and honoured name. He *never did write it;* but how could a son publicly disclaim it, and say my father is a Liar and a Forger? Of course he could *not.* But where he is eternally to be blamed is for ever having let weak-

ness and subserviency come to *that;* when, instead of thanks
for having thrown himself into the breach to save his fiend
father from the crushing disgrace of a full *exposé* of the Mad
House Conspiracy, he found that unscrupulous monster only
wanted him to tell more lies, and forge new springes for his
Victim Mother, he should have unhesitatingly and firmly refused,
and said—No, sir, I have done everything I could, and more than
I ought, to screen you; setting facts, and truth, and my own
feelings, and all justice, at defiance to do so; but if you now
intend to break faith, and go back from all you promised in a
moment of imminent peril, you cannot expect me to write myself
down a Coward or a Villain by deserting and betraying the
Mother, through whose unexampled forbearance and noble self-
abnegation I was alone able to serve you. For had not my poor,
generous Mother accepted *me* as a hostage, you know the QUEEN'S
dominions would not have bribed her to forego the public redress
she was so more than entitled to. But this would have been
honest and true; and how could Sir E——'s son, pupil, and tool,
be either? And, alas! the Bible is right—as the twig is bent, so
will it grow. Poor, poor, unfortunate young martyr! as his
Fiend Father has crushed my life from out its setting, so has
he crushed that young and once bright soul from out its orbit,
and sent it erring through the tenebrous nebula of his own
Avernus. Poor young victim! truly

> " His honour, rooted in dishonour stood,
> And faith, unfaithful! made him falsely true."

For if you only knew his opinion of and feeling towards that
vile Father, you would not wonder that after, through sheer
moral cowardice, having been made to run counter to all his *feelings*
and his whole nature, and play the part of a sort of *Judas tranie
Tartufe!* he should have written in that heart-cry of his, called
" Last Words," that appeared three years ago in the *Cornhill
Magazine.*

" But what will the angels say, when they are looking at me?"

They will tell him perhaps that his Mother pitied even while she
despised him. There *are* some persons who can manage to
love, and yet despise; I cannot, as I told him; for with me contempt is a moral bourne from which no affection ever returns.
But I am *not* angry with him. Oh no, I wish I was; for that
would pass. No, I am not angry with him; I have left him all
I have in the world—not money, for I have none; but all my
pictures, books, bronzes, rare carvings, and rarer historical
enamel portraits, and miniatures, including a most exquisite one
of *la belle Ferronière,* that belonged to FRANCOIS PREMIER, and a
fine miniature of Madame DE MONTESPAN, set in a diamond

bracelet, which had belonged to her son, the Duc DE MAINE! also a fine miniature of the great Lord STRAFFORD, and that most beautiful miniature of Lord BYRON that Lady CAROLINE LAMB left me; my large Sèvres jewelled *Ecrelles*, with a portrait of LOUIS Quinze on it, which he gave to poor MARIE ANTOINETTE when she was Dauphine; and which she gave to the Comte D'ARTOIS (CHARLES DIX), who gave it to his cousin, the Duc DE BOILLON, and he it was left it to my mother. All my *bijouterie* I have also left him, but with a solemn injunction in my will, on pain of GOD's judgment! that he should never desecrate the grave of the Mother he had so *cruelly betrayed*, and inhumanly neglected, by any tombstone, verbiage, or any impious posthumous sentimentalities! in Poems or Magazines.—Amen.

And yet with all my knowledge of and unlimited faith in the diabolical villainy of Sir EDWARD, there is *still* a mystery of iniquity about his unhallowed power (divorced as it is from all affection and respect) over his truly unfortunate Son, that even I cannot fathom, nor even guess at. But I must get to the end as quickly as possible; for much as I have tried to condense this complex tissue of iniquity, which after all is but a drop in the great ocean of it, in which I have been plunged; it would have been quite unintelligible to you, as a stranger to both the actors, and their actions, had I not, in narrating the latter, put you in some degree *au fait* to the former.

Well, the next day, after Miss R——'s semi-nocturnal visit, when without giving me any particulars, she informed me I was to be set at liberty almost immediately, H—— came up, and was more explicit, for he was in a towering passion, fanning himself with a newspaper that he clutched vindictively. "'Pon my word," said he, "those abominable papers are too bad! More especially the Somersetshire ones; to read their abusive tirades, one would really suppose, Lady L——, that instead of being surrounded with every comfort, you had been thrown into a dungeon." "You forget, Mr. H——," said I, "to the impartial public, who are not *paid*, and have no *interest* in thinking otherwise, the infringement upon the liberty of the subject in *any* way, much less in the brutal one of so unwarrantably kidnapping and seizing without judge or jury an inoffensive and defenceless woman, and incarcerating her in a lunatic asylum, is in itself a quite sufficient deed of iniquity— whatever the Sybarite surroundings of the locale may be— to raise a storm of public indignation far more easily evoked than quelled. And you also forget that, take a person nolens volens, and by force, to Buckingham Palace, or to the Tuileries, which is rather more like a palace—and nail down the windows, lock the doors, and put keepers to attend to them, and *presto!* you convert the palace into a prison, and the most terrible of all prisons, a Madhouse." Finding he could get no sympathy from me, as he might have supposed! he began tapping that bay window of a paunch of his, and said he was so ill with all the uproar that was going on, that he was obliged to take "*shugger*" (sugar) in his tea!!!! which he never did but when he was ill! Having stated this highly interesting and physiological fact, he left the room as abruptly as he had entered it. Now really his coming to *me* for sympathy and consolation, on the vituperations of the public against him, was almost as fine a piece of logical and inverse justice as Lord DUNDREARY, in *Punch*, saying in a fury to his wife upon getting his brother's letter, "I tell you what, GEORGINA, if I had known you would have had such a beastht of a brother-in-law as THOM, I would not have married you." Feeling very sure that Mr. L—— would return to the charge, I sat down and wrote him a letter, ready to be given to him when he came. Oh! if we have a Guardian Angel, why did mine desert his post on that day! of all days? I had nearly finished my letter, when that too odious Miss R—— marched in again informing me she had brought my Son down with her again ; then, said I, " you may take him *back* with you again ; but just wait two minutes and my letter will be finished, which I am writing to him, and you can give it to him. " Whereupon this always vulgar, illbred, and unwarrantable person, pounces down her skinny, talonlike hand, seizes my letter, and tears it to pieces. I was indignant at such an impertinent outrage, and ordered her to leave the room. She had scarcely done so, before the door again opened, and in walked Mr. L——, while the door was locked on the outside! The next moment he was kneeling and kissing my feet in a paroxysm of tears—I cannot describe the scene that followed, and I would not, if I could. Enough, that at the end of three hours, he still found me *determined* to seek legal redress, both in the Divorce Court and elsewhere, for the culminating outrage his Father had inflicted upon me. He said he thought his Father would destroy himself, rather than stand the disgrace. I laughed at *that*, and told him not to alarm himself, for that his Father was far too great a coward to die voluntarily, even a coward's death ; he might, indeed, said I, murder either you or me, if he thought he could lay the crime on anyone else, or make it appear that we had committed suicide. And to tell you the truth, I have *no* compassion for that nice sense of honour which only shrinks from the public odium of exposure, but defies GOD, by never recoiling before the commission of any amount of evil doing that money can conceal, or hypocrisy varnish. "Then, mother," said he solemnly and sadly,—"every prospect I have in life is ruined, I never *can* stand the fearful, the horrible exposure of my Father that is inevitable." Here, he had hit the mark ; I leaned back in my chair, irresolute, and he saw it, while he continued kneeling with both my hands in his, and his pale tearful, agonized face, looking up to mine. "But don't you know, don't you see, ROBERT, that the *moment* your Father has cleared this precipice with impunity; then shall I be debarred by 'condonation' from my redress, and left more at his mercy (who has none!) than ever."

"No, no, my own angel darling Mother, then you will bind me to you for ever; he *cannot*, he *dare* not, after owing his salvation to your generosity—prevent your having me to protect, and be devoted to you all my life, and if anything goes wrong in future, you will always have me to appeal to, and protect you. Oh, Mother! if you could but see into my heart, you would see that I would, that I have given up everything to get to you and to be with you. I know I am not worth it, that is, that I *have* been far from worth it, but if you could, darling, make this great, great, noble sacrifice for me— your child—never, never, shall you repent it." After a great deal in the same strain, striking the one chord in my heart that he knew he was *sure* of, till he had brought it into perfect unison with his own wishes, he had conquered. I threw my arms about his neck and said, " Oh, ROBERT, had you asked me to tear my heart out bodily, and give it naked and unguarded into your keeping, it would not be half such a sacrifice as you require of me." " I know it, mother darling, I know it ;" and then, after a couple of the happiest and perhaps the most foolish hours I ever passed in my life, believing—as I firmly did—that out of such a Slough of Despond I had walked into the warm sheltering Paradise of my child's heart, who at least *externally* and in manner was all I could wish, which was in itself a great boon after the coarse, common clay I had so long been used to be knocked and bruised against. When he urged me to go abroad with him, to pass what he called our honeymoon, and to take Miss R——, as he might not be able to get sufficient leave of absence to return with me at the end of three or four months, "Oh! no, not Miss R——," said I, "she is so very antipathic to me. I'll give her any sum of money for any exertions she may have made in getting my incarceration made public, but we shall be so happy without her, and she is such a wet blanket, and a dirty wet blanket too." " Well, that she certainly *is*, and when I first saw her I said to myself, 'Heavens! *can* this be a *friend* of my mother's?' But when she told me all you had done for her, I then knew how it was. She seems to have set her heart upon going abroad with us, and after all she's done, I don't think we could well refuse her." " Well, dear," said I, very much annoyed at this, "you might have let me choose my own evils and not have extended your hospitality to my *bete noire*. But suppose I *do* yield every point to you, in this way; you know I cannot possibly go abroad, whatever arrangements are made, without appointing one Trustee, and that is more easily said than done, as I know of old the great dislike people have to being brought into contact with your Father; knowing that they have either to abandon my rights, or quarrel with him, which before was what drove me to the *pis aller* of appointing the do-nothing-goose, Sir THOMAS CULLUM." After considering a little while, I said : " I have no great faith in public philanthropists, more especially of the Exeter Hall breed; but as he is one of the Commissioners in Lunacy, and knows the whole affair, I wonder if, under the circumstances, as a piece of good Samaritanship, Lord SHAFTESBURY would consent to be my Trustee? for he might be a check upon your Father." "A very good person," said he, "I'll ask him, and let you know to-morrow, darling." So, it being then seven o'clock, and he having to get back for his Father's dinner, left me after this most harrowing day; though I then little dreamed of the red-hot ploughshares there were to come, after being kept full three months in a Fool's Paradise about my son's love and devotion to me; and when I used to chide him for being so demonstrative, even in public places, and say people would think I was some old woman whom he had married for money, he would say, " Oh, but Mother darling, we are not like ordinary Mother and Son ; I love you in every possible way, and then I love you back all the love I've not been let to pay you for years; and then you have suffered *so* much, and borne it so nobly, that you are to me something holy." At other times he would cry out after hugging me, "Mamma," as he always called me, "what I worship in you, is, that with a lion's heart, you are so tender a woman!" All these demonstrations were, of course, music to my ears, and what tended materially to keep me in this Fool's Paradise, was that there was a girl whom he was much attached to (not an English miss, thank GOD), and whom his vile Father was luring him on to suppose he would give him sufficient money to marry, and when I used to see him looking wretched, and thinking it was about her, he'd burst into tears, and throw himself into my arms, saying, " Oh, no! it's not that, Mother, for I declare before GOD, if it were to be made a matter of alternative, which I would give up, her or you, I'd give her up to-morrow, if I might always have you with me." Then, too, a very old and kind benefactor of his, an elderly gentleman, who had shown him much kindness, and whose large means, when ROBERT was a boy, had often atoned for his father's sordid parsimony, wrote to me, saying, " I can answer for the deep love and yearning, dear, dear ROBERT has always had for his Mother; and oh! how sincerely do I rejoice in his happiness now." Add to which my maid was always telling me that FLETCHER, ROBERT'S valet, used to say to her, "Oh! how Mr. L——does adore his Mother. I often surprise him kissing her gloves, and slippers. Poor young gentleman! I never saw a happy face on him till now ; he seems like a natural person now, which he never did with his Father, of whom he is mortally afraid." So you will own that if this was fooling, I was *well* fooled. But I must return to the horrors. The next day, after the first on which I had seen him, Mr. L—— returned to the lodge, and on coming into the room, said, "Well darling, you owe me a million of kisses, for I have good news for you ; SHAFTESBURY consents to being your trustee, so *that's* settled." I thought this exceedingly kind of Lord SHAFTESBURY, as I did not know him personally, and of course wrote to thank him, which note I gave to Mr. L—— to take to town ; and, despite the almost universality of English bearishness and ill-breeding, still as anything in the shape of a gentleman or gentlewoman always answers a letter, more especially such a one as I had written, I was surprised at that evening, and the whole of the next day passing without my receiving any reply ; and I said to Mr. L——, late on the following day, "Are you *sure*, ROBERT, that my note went to Lord SHAFTESBURY?" "I would not trust it to a servant, so I took it myself." At this I felt quite satisfied and did not think any more of the matter. The next day the invasion increased ; I was quite knocked up, and in bed. That vile fellow, ——, came down to see me. I told Miss R—— to say I could not see him, as I was in bed, and I added to her—though he was acting in my interest, I would not see him if I were not. Indeed, a friend of mine, Mrs. T——, told me, after my return from my trapped going abroad, that hearing —— was engaged, she had driven down to Miss R—— at 12 at night, to tell her, for Heaven's sake to be on her guard, that that man, of such notoriously infamous character, retained by Sir E——, did not wreck me. But she having so completely done so, in order, as she thought, to play her own game, replied, like the double distilled ass she is, " Oh, —— is all on Lady L——'s side!" "Oh, Miss R——," said Miss T——, " how can you believe such nonsense as that?"

Well, it appears that with E—— J—— had come down Mr. L——, and Dr. F—— W——, who, I was told, was come on my behalf to counteract—that is, contradict—the statements made by that precious pair of rascals, R—— and H—— T——. "But how," said I, " can he possibly do that when he knows nothing about me—has never seen me, and will only do so for a few minutes ? " Verily they are a nice set, one and all of them, ready to swear a poor victim mad or sane, at a moment's notice, for value received! Shame! shame! That disgusting Miss R—— then began screaming out in her peacock voice, " Now your son wants you to go abroad with him to-morrow." " But I won't and can't," said I ; " I must at least have a week to get some clothes and things." And then this horrid creature made me quite ill with her vulgar bullying manner, and I begged she would leave the room. The dulcifluous Dr. F—— W—— was then sent up to me, as he with more tact than truth expressed it, to know my wishes. I told him that I thought I had done quite enough in yielding to my son's wishes in going abroad at all; and that I did not see why I was to be hurried off in this life and death way, as if *I* had committed a crime, and was to be smuggled out of the country. "Very true," said the amiable Doctor, "and I am sure nothing can be more reasonable than your wish to have a few days to prepare for the journey." He then added, "You are to have, or they are getting you (I don't remember the exact words) a thousand a year, and a house to be furnished for you in town;" which flourishing promise ended in £500, but the solemn assurance from Sir LIAR, E—— J——, and HYDE, that all my debts should be immediately paid, and my debts of honour, before I could get across the Channel was never kept. The dulciferous Dr. W——, after so perfectly agreeing in all I said, then went down, to as perfectly agree with all the opposition said; and was again sent back to urge *their* suit; telling me confidentially that the fact was, that the place was in such an uproar that Sir E—— was terrified; and there would be no peace till the public was assured I was at liberty, and really gone abroad with my son. I may as well here tell you, that such was the honourable estimation Sir L—— was held in by the said public, that people fully believed I was sent abroad to be made away with; and hence, among *many others*, the atrocious lie, that I was accompanied by a *relation of my own! M—— R——, by my own special request!* Whereas, as I discovered, like all the rest, too late, this wretch was only sent as a Spy on me and my Son —upon the Jesuitical plan *of triplets*, and as "own correspondent" to Sir LIAR, to whom she used to write *every* day from the programme *he* had given her, the blackest lies, for him to read to people :—such for instance, as that I had been very violent and unmanageable till I had arrived in Paris, when I became calmer! the real truth being, that I was *so* exhausted, in body and mind from all I had gone through, that I could scarcely move or speak, but used to say, lying down, while my son sat beside me, my hand clasped in his, that I felt so grateful to GOD for his being restored to me that I could almost forgive the relentless author of my life-long misery, and cruelly exceptional persecutions; but that at all events now I'd try and forget him and them, and think of nothing but the present and the future. Well, Dr. F—— W——, finding he could not move me from my resolve of not being smuggled out of the country like a felon, sent up the only person who could fool me, my son. And when he told me what it would entail upon him, if he could not succeed in doing his father's bidding, why then I yielded; and having been brought to Mr. H——'s stronghold on Wednesday the 22nd of June, 1858, at 7 p.m., I left it on Saturday, July the 17th, 1858, at 3 p.m., by almost an equal degree of treachery, falsehood, and springeing. Poor little MARY H—— cried so violently, that I was really grieved to leave her, and felt quite selfish in going (as I then thought) to be happy, when she who had been for three weeks my one sole Star in the Desert was left so unhappy. Mrs. H—— said the whole affair had made her *us*band *hill;* I said I thought he had been always HILL; while *he* said he had never suffered so much in his life ; the uproar that had been made had played the deuce with him. "I told you it would, Mr. H——, the day you *forced* me to come here ; why did you not listen to me?" "And then," said he, "my daughter MARY is breaking her heart, and I have got, I'm sure, a confirmed liver complaint from it." "Then," said I, "you must leave off '*shugger*,' it is the worst thing in the world for the liver." Dr. OILY GAMMON R—— told me, after my return, that H—— had been on his knees, imploring him to have pity on his ten children, and not ruin him. The valiant Doctor, who literally could not, or would not say Boo! to a goose, or he might have had *beau jeu* with H——, pretends he said to him, "You should have thought of these before. You had no mercy upon Lady L—— when you dragged her to your asylum in that iniquitous manner." However, after my departure Brentford became too hot for him, and he removed to London, where, between him and the *rest* in whose power he, of course, was completely, I understand Sir LIAR was completely beggared with hush-money ; not with my tremendous debts, which, at the end of 20 years' *ceaseless* persecutions, and conse-quent onerous law expenses, amounted to the mighty sum of £4,500, which, when at last at the point of the sword, *alias* the *writ*, that generous and honourable man was *compelled* to pay ; he did so by disgorging some of my own money. Upon this memorable and broiling 17th of July, 1858, from 3 to 7 p.m., I had to drive all over London in quest of ready-made things, and then go to 'Farrance's Hotel' to eat a hurried dinner, and after from Belgrave-square to the London Bridge Station, so that I was really quite worn out when at 11 o'clock at night I found myself in bed at the 'Lord Warden Hotel,' Dover, from whence we did not cross to Calais till Monday, the 19th, all *newspapers* being *carefully* kept *out of my way ;* and, indeed, I was both too happy and too tired to ask for any, which, of course, was *precisely* what was calculated upon. Abroad, I can only suppose that all my letters were intercepted by that vile Miss R—— in her capacity of own correspondent to Sir LIAR, as Mrs. CLARKE told me she had forwarded innumerable ones ; and, on my return, I found duplicates, recapitulating their painful contents, and alas! too late warnings, as warnings generally are. " For I told thee so " the Fiend ever whispers, when the deed is done! At Bordeaux I got a letter from JUDAS H——, in which the following audacious and asinine passage occurred, "Sir EDWARD is *quite* changed, his only wish is to render your life in future as happy as possible." To which I replied, " Yes, no doubt, for it is a patent fact in natural history that the leopard is in the habit of changing its spots at a moment's notice." A few nights after this H—— humbug, ROBERT was brought some letters from England at the Opera, one of which he no sooner read than bursting into a perfect agony of tears, he rushed out of the box. I, of course, went after him, when that beast, Miss R——, caught hold of my dress to prevent my following him, saying, "Augh, shure, he's often in dat way," as if she had known him all her life, and had been his *bonne d'enfant*. I could not find him; and when that night I went to kiss him, and wish him good-night, I found him pacing his room in a state of distraction, with his hands to his head, exclaiming, " What *does* my father think I'm made of! what can he suppose I am ? " And upon another occasion, though not so fearfully shaken, he appeared in a greater rage; his vile father had written him a furious letter about the scandalous expenses of our journey ! "As if," said ROBERT, "I was a dishonest courier; and talks of withdrawing his patronage ! from me, as if I was some beggar he had picked up in the street!" " Well dear," said I, " you should keep a strict account of the expenditure ; enclose your father all the bills, and ask him if he knows of any way in which five persons can travel for nothing in a country where everything now is fabulously dear ? " For even at Luchon at the *end* of the season, after leaving the *Hotel de Bonne Maison* as being too expensive, they made us pay 500 francs a week for the Châlet we had, for which in the season Mme. DE ROTHSCHILD had paid 1000. Often and often, when I saw the poor boy in these dreadful paroxysms of mingled rage and despair, I implored him on my knees to confide in me, and I would *help* him, if it were even against myself, for I could bear anything and everything, but to feel and find out that my own child, for whom I had sacrificed everything, and in whom I had garnered up all my hopes, was deceiving me ! And who *can* you trust if not your own mother? But no, the chronic habits of terror and subterfuge were too strong ! even when stung or goaded into making me little half-confidences, from which no one, as I told him, could give sound advice, as the very point that is kept from them is in all probability the turning one, which would alter their whole opinion and counsel. But his terror of his vile father was so great, and now added to it, that of that " beastly disgusting old Spy," as he called her, that even in the heart of the Pyrenees, if he did unburden himself in the least to me, it was in a whisper; and he would turn pale, and look furtively around, as if the very birds of the air would carry his words back to Park-lane, or Downing-street. Poor young martyr! poor young martyr! But all the tortures he was then enduring were worthy of the Fiend-Father, who when the poor boy had had a fearful, and nearly fatal, fever at Lucca—took no note of whether he lived or died, only to storm about the expense of the Doctors !!! Yet this is the loathsome wretch! to whom he allowed the impious dedication to "Lucile" to appear, and blaspheme about his "loved! and honoured name!! and his *gentle* kindness to him as a child !!" And this is the Father for whom he could so cruelly and treacherously sacrifice the Mother who *had* sacrificed everything, and every chance of redress for him, and whom he professed to adore, in a way that might have deceived the Recording Angel himself. And worse still! Miss R——, whom he so loathed and detested, that old Spy, as he called her—was the parasite he could afterwards cabal with against his Mother, to steal those letters of his infamous Father's, which I had entrusted to that creature the day I was kidnapped at H—— T-—'s; but in *that* they did not succeed, as you shall hear presently. So much for that paralysis of the conscience, moral cowardice, which is at once the germ and hotbed of every vice. It was not until I had been thus far springed upon, and thus far on the journey, that after writing to know if all my debts of honour had been paid, as so *solemnly promised* before I could get across the channel, and the deed drawn up, settling that beggarly £500 a year on me for *my* life, that I got a letter from that precious rascal, Mr. —— ——, coolly telling me that everything was at a standstill, *till* I had appointed a trustee !!! I sent for Mr. L——, and pointing to the paragraph, said "What does this fresh shuffle mean? did you not explicitly tell me at Inverness Lodge that Lord SHAFTESBURY had consented to be my trustee? and that you *yourself* took my note of thanks to him? to which I have never from that day to this received any answer?" He turned red and pale alternately, stuttered, stammered, and said, "Did not H—— tell you?" "Tell me what?" said I; "when and where could I have seen him, to tell me anything?—when I was hurried out of the country like a condemned felon. Of course, that your father, and Mr. —— ——, might have the whole arena to themselves, to concoct their unscrupulous lies and plots." *This* was the first terrible wrench my affection, that is my esteem for, and confidence in, my son got. A few days after, I saw an advertisement in the *Times*, from that low swindling publisher ——, of Paternoster-row, of a cheap railway edition of a book of mine called '—— ——,' which at the time it came out, two years before, Sir LIAR had left no stone unturned to get crushed and abused. Now a Mr. IRONSIDE had undertaken to sell *one* of my books to

—— for a re-issue, and knowing the apathetic hand-over-head way English people do other people's business, I gave Mr. IRONSIDE a list of the books he was *not* to allow to go into a railway edition, and another list of books of which I had *not* the copyrights, and '—— ——,' was *first* upon the interdicted list. Seeing this barefaced swindle, I sent for Mr. L——, knowing how potential a man's name always is with English blackguards, and I said, " Will you just write two lines to that fellow ——, saying, ' Sir,—My mother having seen in the *Times* of the 26th of September (1858), an advertisement of yours re-issuing a novel of hers, entitled "—— ——," which Mr. IRONSIDE had so expressly forbidden you to do, she wishes to know by whose, and what authority you have now done so?—I am, sir, your obedient servant,

" ' R—— B—— L——.' "

" " Ah ! " said the young gentleman, " my father has written to me about this re-issue, and says you have broken faith with him about that book in re-issuing it." " How broken faith with him ? " said I. " How could that be when I have never had any communication with him upon that or any other subject? I merely interdicted ——'s re-issuing that book, because I could get better terms for it elsewhere. So pray ask your father *how* I could have broken faith with *him* about it; and how angry I am at ——'s barefaced swindle! and pray go and write that letter to —— directly." I may as well here tell you while I think of it, that part of their plan was to get me to go back and live with Sir LIAR for a short time to patch up his character, and throw dust in the eyes of the public, which is all that is ever required on the score of English morality. Had I been such a glorious fool as to do this, of course he could have poisoned me off comfortably out of hand, and then written a touching *In Memoriam* on me in Mr. HUMBUG DICKENS's " *All the Year Round.*" For that vile Miss R——, one day at Luchon, had the imbecility and the effrontery to bring me a letter from her employer, from which that meanest of all villains had ordered her to read out the following *unique* in the annals of humbug paragraph : " Try and soften Lady L——'s heart, by reminding her of the time when I was so devoted to her "!!!

" Dear, now, do *tink* of your own interest, and tell me what I shall write back to Sir EDWARD." " One word will do," said I, "the word ' When ? ' "

In my dreadful dilemma of being without a trustee—not to leave them any pretext for keeping the poor people out of their money, I had written to Dr. OILY GAMMON R—— to know if *he* would be my trustee? Not certainly from choice, as I never have any but Hobson's choice ; but because he was already *au fait* to the last Madhouse Conspiracy, and knew all the *dramatis personæ.* He wrote me back a most oleaginous letter, accepting the office, and praising Mr. L—— up to the skies, with one of those double barrelled compliments which professionally he was in the habit of bestowing upon my lord and my lady—*i.e.*, saying " He is a noble fellow, worthy of the mother who bore him." No, verily ; *she* is *not* a coward ; and for all the kingdoms of the earth could neither lie away a person's life, repay good with evil, or cringe to infamy in high places ; nor pander to treachery and injustice. Though as FALSTAFF was not only witty himself, but the cause of wit in others ; so Sir EDWARD is not only false, treacherous, and infamous, but is the cause of falsehood, treachery, and infamy in others. Yet, thank GOD, neither by bribery nor intimidation, has he ever, or will he ever, be able to mould me to his purposes ; and hence his implacable persecution, and his poisoned treacherous arrows that always fly in *darkness*, and from an ambush. When Mr. L—— returned with his dispatch to C——, he put it into my hand, saying " Will that do ? " It began : " SIR,—Lady B—— L—— having seen in *The Times*," &c., &c. " No," I said, " it will *not* do ; I told you to say my mother having seen, &c., &c., that he fully might know that I had a son, and therefore conclude, however erroneously, that he would protect me." At this he left the room, and I felt so angry and heart-stricken, that I wrote him an indignant note, reproaching him with having lured and springed me abroad, merely to patch up his father's character, which, sooth to say, was rather past mending. Upon the receipt of this, for truth to evil-doers is the most unpardonable of all crimes, *car ce n'est que la verité qui blesse*, the young gentleman having of course had his *orders* (and when did this pious ÆNEAS ever dare to disobey any order of his loved !!! and honoured !!! father, " from pitch-and-toss up to manslaughter ? "), sent for post horses and set off to Toulouse, on his return to Paris, leaving his Mother, now nothing more could be done with her, and the bubble was beginning to burst, to find her way home as she could. Certainly he did leave his man FLETCHER to attend upon mê, who kept saying to WILLIAMS (my maid) the whole journey, " 'Pon my soul, it's too, too bad ; I did not think Mr. L—— *could* have acted so by his Mother—whom I know he loves—merely from fear of that old villain Sir EDWARD." When I found Mr. L—— gone, without a word, without a line, my short dream all shattered and shimmering about me ! and a cold, black, unfathomable abyss before me,—never shall I forget the first petrifying yet bewildering agony—the severing, as it were, of body and soul—that I felt, and which I am certain must be what one feels when the real severing of them by death comes. For hours I seemed turned to stone, and could not shed a tear, till I saw, sitting under the trees opposite our windows, in her little carriage, a poor little lame girl about thirteen, who used to sit there begging. She had a little, pale, melancholy face, with imploring eyes, that seemed to say, "*Pour l'amour de Dieu!*" for she never asked in words. ROBERT had given her a five-franc piece one day, and came into me with the tears streaming down his cheeks, and said, "Oh, Mother, can you give me any warm wraps for her? she is so cold and so thinly clad." How I loved the poor fellow at that moment—so much good feeling was so *un*-Bulwerish, and so *un*-Lyttonian. I gave him all he wanted, and he then flung his arms round my neck, and said, "How good you are to me, darling; anyone else would have laughed at me." "Then they must be thorough wretches if they did," said I. Upon seeing his poor little *protégée* looking up wistfully, that cold, gloomy November day, after he was gone, I put on my bonnet, and went down to her. Her first question was for "Monsieur"—for he was her idol; no one, she said, had ever been so kind, or so gentle to her. When I told her he was gone, and would not return, she cried bitterly. Her name was JEANNE HESTIER. I said, "JEANNE, would you like to be taken out of the cold and clothed, and taught, and live entirely *avec les bonnes sœurs a l'Hospice?*" She clasped her hands and said, "Oh, that would be too good—but what would my mother say?" who took all the money people gave her at the baths (and indeed I had trouble enough with the worthless, grasping mother after). "Oh, never mind, I'll settle that," said I, and I took the pole of her little carriage and drew her to the convent, where I consigned her to the *Mère Supérieure*, paying the first year in advance, and sufficient besides for her "*necessaire*"—have done so ever since, and shall do so as long as I live; and as it is only £20 a year, I hope and trust Mr.—— won't leave poor JEANNE to starve when I am dead, as I send the money every six months, through his old Luchon Doctor, Dr. PEJOT. It is so *pleasant* to have his inquiries about "*le jeune homme charmant Monsieur votre fils.*" Oh, what a bitter! bitter! sting, life is to some of us. Well, when I arrived in Paris, I still made a last effort to save this wretched young victim from himself. I sent a note to the hotel, where he always put up, to tell him not, after what *he* and *he* alone (for no one else could have done it) had trapped me into, to let us part in such a manner; for if he did, nothing should induce me ever to see him again. He came, but the hideous KATE R—— was in the room, and his manner was cold and constrained. To get rid of her (for she always stuck to us like a leech), I sent her off on a wild goose chase to GALIGNANI'S. I then implored him only to be candid with me, and tell me all, no matter how bad it was, or what his orders were to do against me; I would not only freely forgive him, but help him, for, as I said before, I could bear all things; but to feel *he* was deceiving me, and I should not at all mind what I suffered, or even try to get redress for any outrages or insults from his father, and his father's tools; if I could be only *certain* that my own child was merely playing a part against me, and *not* doing so in his own heart; much as I deprecated such expedient duplicity, and which, to save my life, I could not resort to myself He flung himself at my feet, hiding his face in my lap, and in such an agony of hysterical sobs, that I really was quite frightened. But not one word could I get out of him. As there is no courage like a coward's for rashness, when pushed to desperation, so I suppose there is no obstinacy like a weak vacillator's, when they have been pushed to take the Curtius' leap into the gulf of determination. At dinner, the Spy being there, he again congealed into a proper B—— L——ish degree of frigidity, and talked of this, that and the other, *sachant sans doute, que la bete noire R——, etait la faisant son courier, et dressant son procès verbal—pour son barbe bleu de pere.* Then he said how sorry he was to leave beautiful Luchon, which was the most lovely place he had ever seen. And that poor little lame girl—her face haunted him—he must send her something, "You need not, at least just now," said I, "for I thought you would be glad of it, so I've provided for your child." "Provided for her! how?" I then told him I had deposited her with my friends, the Sisters of Charity, at the Hospice, where both she and her health would be taken care of. At this he drew up, with an air of pomposity that was almost worthy of "my father," and said—while Miss R——'s hideous, toad-like eyes were fixed upon him, "Those sort of things are all very well, if people have large fortunes." "Well," I broke in, "it will neither come out of your father's private fortune (whatever that may really be, it is so magnified to the public, and so contradicted to his family), nor out of his £5,000 a year as Colonial Secretary; and, by doing without something else, I have no doubt I shall be able to manage £20 a year, even out of my splendid income."

But all my pleasures were still to come! The good people of Taunton, when they heard I was to return safe and sound, wanted to give me a triumphal entry from the station. But upon my unhappy son's account, I wrote to Mrs. CLARKE to say how grateful I felt, and always should feel, to them for their great kindness and zeal on my behalf; but that they would greatly add to their kindness, if they would allow me to return to them as quietly as possible, as I was far from well. On my return, I found duplicates of the intercepted letters, which had not reached me abroad · they were all to the same purport, and in the same strain, viz., that it was natural for me to believe in my son, but imploring me not to *trust* him; as "the world paints him in the same colours as his father—black, and very black." And in confirmation of this, they enclosed me two infamous letters, tissues of the *grossest* falsehoods, which had appeared in *The Times* on Saturday, July the 17th, 1858, the very day I was taken from H——'s stronghold, and hurried off without breathing time to Dover, which letters bore my son's signature! But knowing the unscrupulous use his Ruffian of a Father made of his name, I tried to hope that they were a concoction of his and L——'s, and wrote of course to JUDAS H——, and my OILY GAMMON of a trustee, Dr. R——, about them. Mr. H—— of course "very much disapproved" of these letters! but thought it better—no doubt he was paid for so doing —to let them die away, by not taking any notice of them! a nice way of defending a client truly! While Dr. OILY GAMMON "was quite shocked and startled at them, and would certainly have contradicted every false statement contained in them, *had he been my trustee at the time (!!!)* and he had quite dreaded the effect they would have on me when they came to my knowledge!" Yet the sneaking toady and loathsome double-dealer, being perfectly cognisant of them at the time, could, with all his pretended friendship and sympathy! let me leave England with this mine of cowardly lies exploding after me, and continue his horrible hypocrisy by writing to me that my son "was a noble fellow"! *Il parènt en ce cas la que, noblesse! n'obligèant pas!* I was also sent some Hertford Papers with a letter from that vile wretch, Miss R——, saying that "she was bound to say (no doubt of it) that Sir EDWARD —— had never been unkind to me! and that from the *representations made to him (!!!!!)* he could not have done otherwise than send me to Mr. H——'s *establishment!* which had been done solely for the benefit of my health." The attorney H——, signing himself "Lady BULWER LYTTON'S Solicitor," was, of course, *bound* to tell the same lies. But the Hertford Papers opened a perfect battery of indignation upon that vile Miss R——, saying—who could have but the worst opinion of a person who, for ten days had printed statements in not only the Hertford but London papers, that *nothing* could exceed Sir EDWARD ——'s cruelty to, and persecution of me for years, which she could vouch for before his culminating Conspiracy of the Madhouse, and that out of Hell there were not two other such demons as he and L——. And then! in the short space of half an hour after her first interview with these men, she writes to say he had never been unkind to me! Why, they *could* only say that she was a bribed perjurer, and that if anything *could* damage Sir EDWARD more in public opinion, it would be her present sudden and contradictory statements respecting him. As for Mr. H——! solicitors are a proverb for *their* elastic consciences. But it is the old story in all cases of the wicked strong against the innocent weak. Sir WALTER RALEIGH, it was arranged *before-*

hand, was to be condemned; therefore, vain were his cloud of
witnesses, his legions of facts, and his eloquence of truth. Just
as, of course, Prime Ministers never are, under the most glaring
and palpable of facts, to be found guilty in cases of *crim. con.*
Why should they, with secret service money and unlimited patronage at their command? I remember that very clever, but intensely
unprincipled literary man, Dr. MAGINN, as most literary men
that I have had the misfortune to know *are*, telling me the
clever dirty work he did in Lord MELBOURNE'S and that vile
Mrs. NORTON'S Trial; how *he* packed the Jury, and how
he invalidated the testimony of the only witness they were
afraid of—a footman, by worming out all his evidence,
and sending it to her Counsel, and making the man so
beastly drunk at the eleventh hour at a public house,
"The Chequer's" at Westminster, that when he was called into
Court it completely invalidated his evidence! And he also gave
me chapters and verses of the *exact* sums of money—Baronetcies
and civil service appointments—he had had to distribute in the
higher quarters; old MELBOURNE sticking out more about the
money than anything, but sending Sir JOSEPH YORKE to close with
his demands at 7 o'clock on the morning of the Trial. But
because MAGINN was a high Tory, the sapient public of course
would never suspect *him* of doing dirty work for a Whig Premier.
Yet this unscrupulous fellow, dining at my house at Bath at the
time, showed me two articles he had written upon this Trial
simultaneously, one, for the Tory *John Bull* and *Standard*, making
Mrs. NORTON out ten times more scarlet than the Lady of
Babylon; the other for a Whig organ *proving* her to be purer
than unturned snow! which is the way Literature and Politics
are conducted in this country. And my miserable lot in life
having thrown me chiefly among Political and Literary Magnates,
I have no hesitation in saying that *all* the misery and crime in
this country (where—despite sermons—schools—refuges and
reformatories they are *ever frightfully on the increase*), originate in
the Stygian vices and blasphemous hypocrisy! of these two great
motive powers. And have we not just been edified with another
signal example of English virtue! and above all, English justice!
in high places, in the Trial of "O'KANE *versus* O'KANE and
PALMERSTON," where you perceive it was *Mr. O'Kane's friends!!*
that negotiated the compromise! as poor dear Lord PALMERSTON
could have no possible interest in the matter!—Oh dear no! so it
was solely for Mr. O'KANE'S interest that he should accept Lord
PALMERSTON'S money, offered by *his* O'KANE'S friends! and as Mrs.
O'KANE had been a maid of Lady JOCELYN'S, and therefore had the
run of Cambridge House, it's not likely that a man of Lord
PALMERSTON'S Cato-like virtue ever even looked at her. So
the superannuated Joseph came out pure and spotless!

(as most men are) amid the plaudits of a properly crammed court, dear COCKBURN having no doubt, *sub rosa*, played the manager, and "animated the whole," even to inspiring *Mr. O'Kane's friends* with the ways and means to inspire O'KANE with a suitable idea of his own interests! Verily the force of humbug can no farther go! On my return to all these agreeable, perhaps not exactly, surprises, I had also the pleasure of finding that none of my debts of honour were paid, despite the solemn promises of all concerned that they were to be, before I crossed the Channel. Only JUDAS H—— had been sent down in hot haste to Taunton to throw dust in the people's eyes by paying the *tradespeople* here, who were in no hurry to be paid, and whom I would much rather have paid myself on my return, when cordially thanking them all for their unanimous and active zeal, for they had even felt in their *pockets* for me, and told Mrs. CLARKE that two or three thousand pounds, or more, should be instantly raised if wanted for law expenses. The only person who had *not* sent in his bill was a Quaker upholsterer, who was owed £5. This turned out a very fortunate circumstance for me, as you will hear presently. After this homœopathic gold-dust throwing at Taunton, Sir LIAR began *a son ordinaire*, going back from *every* promise, when he thought the storm had a little blown over, and what he more particularly stood out about most resolutely, was insisting that that beggarly £500 a year should not be settled upon me for my life, but only for *his*. Whereupon the admirable Mr. E—— J—— told him that if that at least was not done, I should of course proclaim the whole affair, and bring an action for false imprisonment, &c., &c. So that it was at the eleventh hour, four days after my return, that it was at length done ; upon which Dr. OILY GAMMON R——, my valiant trustee, wrote me a most heroic piece of braggadocia, that he would not leave the room till the deed was executed, signed, and duly attested. But by this time, not believing one word any of them said, I sent my copy of this deed to a barrister of my acquaintance, Mr. HENRY COLE, to know if it were a quibble or a fresh *swindle*. He said no, it was stringent and *en regle*, and about a month after its execution JUDAS H—— wrote to me saying Miss R—— and E—— J—— had written, and called innumerable times on him at his office in Ely-place, to try and make him give up the original of that document *to them;* no doubt E—— J—— having promised his friend Sir LIAR that if he'd *only* sign that deed, to humbug me and the public a little more, he (E—— J——) would swindle H—— out of it in some way or other, under pretence of looking at it, and then destroy it. And JUDAS H—— made a tremendous merit to me of his fidelity in not giving it up ; to which I wrote him back word: "Clearly not, Mr. H—— ; you have got all you were to get for selling me, and for your lies to the Hertford and other papers about being *bound* to say that infamous man, Sir EDWARD H——, had never been unkind to me. And of course you were not such a fool as to risk being struck off the Rolls for such an overt breach of trust as the giving up the original of that deed would have been." This reminded me to tell Dr. R—— to get my two letters (those two letters of Sir LIAR'S) from that vile Miss R——. When I told him about my going abroad in the full belief that Lord SHAFTESBURY was my trustee, he, who is Lord SHAFTESBURY'S Physician, said that in the first place he had never been asked, and never got my note, and in the next, if he had, he would have declined, his horror of Sir EDWARD —— was so great. So much for his philanthropy. Mr. L—— having returned to England about his own business with his father, and finding that after solemnly promising poor Lady BLACKBURNE the interest of the £400 she had generously lent me when I was starved out at the Revolution of Geneva in 1846, which interest she never would accept from me, I wrote to Mr. L—— to know if it were possible that in the teeth of all truth he had written those two letters, with his signature to them, which had appeared in the *Times* the day I left England, and which such care was taken I should not see. And also as he had so solemnly promised that I should appeal to *him* if anything went wrong in future ; and I found Dr. R——(as was his bounden duty), though always more than agreeing with me in everything, never saw, or insisted upon any compact being fulfilled, and was worse than none as a trustee. I must depend upon him in common honour and common decency to see that Lady BLACKBURNE, who had acted so kindly and generously by me, should be paid the interest of her money, and all my other debts of honour also *immediately* paid. To this, the young gentleman, who now had his papa, and his papa's cane ! to lean over him, and see that he did his lessons properly (what in mathematics is called a *Crocodile*, I suppose), boldly replied, that " he *had* written those letters,—and that as for Lady BLACKBURNE, she must recollect that in *law !* she could claim *nothing*, and must therefore be contented with the principal without the interest ! (though bear in mind the interest had been solemnly promised to her by *the whole gang*)—and as to taking any proceeding against his father, if I *had no respect for family ties* (*this* from *him* to *me*), that at all events he hoped that I would at least have some respect for the name he (Mr. L——) inherited "! To which I wrote back—" GOD forgive you—you poor unfortunate young man, but as you have every reason to be heartily ashamed of ' the name you inherit ' ! take my advice, and say as little about it as possible, and try before it is too late to act so that *your* children may not have equal cause to be ashamed of the name *they* inherit." You may suppose that by

this t'me I had my quietus! and could not be more wounded and
disgusted. After that contemptible sneak and double-dealer Dr.
R—— had been for *weeks* writing me lying excuses about Miss
R—— not returning me that cheek-biting'and other letter, which
he *knew* to be lies; I received the following charming effusion
from Mr. L——, and to rejoice my mother's heart the more it
came on New Year's Day! and showed me *he* was still doing his
father's dirty work in concert with that vile wretch Miss R——,
whom I had forbidden to ever again darken my doors, if she was
fifty times turned penniless into the streets of London, or any
other place.

"Dear mother, what is this Miss R——tells me about some
letters of my father to you? Surely there was a broad understanding that all your papers (!!) were to be given up to him."
My reply to this disgusting and too brutal piece of audacity,
bearing the stamp of Sir LIAR's cloven foot upon every word,
was to send a gentleman to town to go to Sir RICHARD MAYNE,
who gave him a police force, with which he went to that vile
wretch, Miss R——, and got the letters at last! while to Mr.
L—— I wrote—"As it is not in my nature to love what I could
not esteem, all intercourse must cease between us."—To get that
£1,000, that the gentleman on the Stock Exchange so kindly
lent me, when I had been turned out of my cottage, *he* had to
send a man with a writ to dear E—— J——, who had the nomi-
nal paying of those debts; because, you see, it would not do on
my account to have lying, swindling, or any other villainy brought
directly home to that great man, Sir LIAR! like the villainous and
atrocious lie worthy of him, or of any of his literary gang—that
from the *representations made* to him, *he* could not have done
otherwise than incarcerate me at H——'s. Well, this man,
E—— J——, tried to bully, saying, "No, my good fellow, what
can you do? Surely you'd never think of arresting me, or Sir
EDWARD, for a debt, which in law we might dispute." "Shouldn't
I, Mr. J——," said he, pulling the writ out of his pocket, "you
either instantly give me a cheque for £1,000, which I don't leave
your house *without*, or I instantly serve this writ upon you." So
the *honourable* Q.C. preferred giving the cheque to having the
writ served on him! and the gentleman who had lent me the
money, kindly returned me from the Insurance Office some £50
odd, on the policies I had been paying for seven years,—they
being for life although I had only borrowed the money for
ten years. About this time, Dr OILY GAMMON R—— began
being tremendously civil and *prevenant* to me; he and his wife
sending me Dresden china, and engravings, for which I had no
room, my walls being covered with good pictures. I did not
dream at that time that this smooth-tongued sneaking J——, was
actively enlisted to cheat me out of the copy-right of that book

(Sir LIAR's little bit of *entr'acte* dirty work, while I was safely out of the country), for which I have never received sixpence, or got the slightest redress;—but *more* injustice, as you shall hear. But although I did not know this then, yet I am so fully aware that English people are never commonly civil; and much less never *give* even a used postage stamp without some sordid or selfish motive; that I began to puzzle my brains as to what this sudden civility could mean? I must say, all the good that is to be found in the English character, is among the middle class, and this arises more from their strong commercial instinct, than anything else; they will give an apple, where they are perfectly sure of getting an orchard, or perhaps two; but the upper and lower classes, invariably swindle—or at least *try* to swindle—you out of the orchard, without even giving you an apple-pip for it. Like a poor fool, I went to town, and made an appointment with Dr. OILY GAMMON to go to Mr. C——'s in Paternoster-row, at nine in the morning; despite this matutinal hour, Mr. C—— had had his telegram to keep out of the way, and he was out. OILY GAMMON then went through the farce of writing some bosh to C——, telling his substitute in the shop that he particularly required an answer by the four o'clock post at latest. At four p.m. OILY GAMMON brought me C——'s reply in triumph! which was, that he had *my* authority in my own handwriting, in a note written to Mr. IRONSIDE two years before, to re-issue my novel of "Cheveley!" "Cheveley!" who on earth is talking of "Cheveley"? surely Dr. R——, you would not have made such a ridiculous mistake; when even this morning in C——'s shop, I was reiterating it to you that it was "Very Successful." To say nothing of my having written to you, so *much* on the subject. Then *much* against his will, I made Dr. OILY GAMMON write to C—— to say this; to which that fellow gave the barefaced lie, that he had Mr. IRONSIDE's authority to publish "Very Successful." *This* I *know* to be a black lie! for when I was abroad, Mr. IRONSIDE was so astonished at seeing the book advertised in the teeth of his, and my, prohibition, that he wrote to Mr. H—— to inquire about it, as he was sure I would be very angry when I heard it. That double distilled rascal, liar, and perjurer, wrote back word that it was *all right*, as *I myself* had given C—— permission to re-issue it!!!! Indignant at this, I made Mr. OILY GAMMON write to Mr. IRONSIDE, that he might state to *him* again in writing, what I have just told you, and which he had written a short time before to another gentleman! which letter *I have*. As my grinding poverty is always putting spokes in my wheel (and that is *why I have been always kept poor*), I could not afford to remain in London, either at the houses of fine friends, or at an hotel, so that I returned here, begging OILY GAMMON to let me know Mr. IRONSIDE'S answer, which finding he did *not* do, in the course of five weeks, I wrote to him to know what reply he had received, and to beg he would send me Mr. IRONSIDE'S letter. To this the contemptible wretch wrote back word that he had *lost* Mr. IRONSIDE'S letter, but that all he (IRONSIDE) had said was, that "really, it was so long ago (two years), that he could not remember anything about it"!!! Upon this I made a solicitor of this town write to Dr. R——, saying that after all the contradictory and palpably false statements that had been made to me about that book, it was a great pity that instead of sending *me* Mr. IRONSIDE'S letter at once, as he was in duty bound, he should have lost it, and sent me *no reply at all*, till I had written to him on the subject at the end of five weeks, as both circumstances had a very awkward appearance for him (Mr. R——). Whereupon Mr. OILY GAMMON (for weak cowards are invariably *false to all parties*, themselves included) suddenly and miraculously *found* Mr. IRONSIDE'S letter, and instead of its being (as stated by Dr. R——) only two lines, to say it was so long ago he could not remember, it was a long letter (which I have) of four sides, crossed, on large old-fashioned Bath post paper, such as was used in the days of franking. In this letter he recapitulated *all* he had previously stated in his former letter, of his surprise at the re-issue of the book, and his writing to Mr. H——, to inquire about it, and that lying rascal's answer, stating that it was "all right," I myself having given C—— permission to re-issue it; and Mr. IRONSIDE concluded by saying that my statement was correct to the letter, and that C—— was such. . . .

Armed with this *fresh* proof of the fraud that had been practised upon me, I again went to London, and went to Mr. H—— C——, at his chambers in Brick-court, showed him all the documents I had on the subject, and asked him if he could recommend a good sharp solicitor (honest, I feared, there was none), who would immediately bring an action against C——? That I was quite aware that, as a married slave, *I* could not bring one, or get any redress against my lord and master's infamy : but that by making the book over to what one of the law's charming fictions call "a next friend," I could do so. Mr. C—— said it was a most scandalous shame, and he would recommend me to a clever solicitor, who he thought would settle it (he did, indeed), a Mr. H—— (which may be considered as the generic name of the whole tribe), of Regent-street. This fellow was the image of NAPOLEON the *First*, so I did not doubt his *capacity*—nor, perhaps, his unscrupulousness. As all London knew of the Madhouse Conspiracy then, Mr. JOHN H—— (as I told him I wished his name had been TOM, as a Tomahawk was what I wanted for my enemies) found out many truths about Sir LIAR and E—— J——

deserving hanging, and was urgent, nay importunate, with me, to bring an action against H—— and the rest of them (of *course*, for that would have been a feather in the H——'s cap, or tail, and gold in his crop), but I told him for my truly unfortunate son's sake, I could not, or rather would not; but that he must go to work forthwith about C——.

He then asked me what Judge I would like it tried before? adding, " I would recommend the Chief Justice, Sir ALEXANDER COCKBURN, for he is a friend of mine." Good heavens! said I, if you want to ruin me outright, you will not mix him up in the affair, or let him know anything about it. Now, you must know that although COCKBURN always says I am the worst-used woman in England, so have all my husband's doers of dirty work for that matter ; he and Sir L. were at Cambridge together, and in their green and salad days—when the little carrotty, briefless barrister, who had nothing to eat but his terms, except when he dined with us—Sir L. used to lend him money when he was intriguing with some tradesman's wife, whom he called " CLARA," and by whom he had his bastard son and daughter, whom he has at least the redeeming points of acknowledging and well-providing for—and I respect him for it. But you comprehend, this having been the state of affairs between him and Sir L., they, like literary vice and politics, have their laws and amenities, which require that dirty work and backstair services should always be paid in kind, and however dislike and contempt may be and are in the ascendant in private, homage, deference and friendship (?) is *de riguéur* in public. And as astronomers say that it takes two-and-twenty years for a ray of light to reach the earth from Sirius, the Dog Star ; so I suppose it takes two-and-twenty centuries for a ray of conscience to penetrate such a lawyer as COCKBURN, or, indeed, most men's brains. " Humph !" said H——. " Well, I'd rather have a case tried by COCKBURN than any Judge on the bench." " You might," said I, " but mine is such a hard case that I don't want it made harder." Well, not to bore you longer than need be, Mr. H—— having started with the *greatest* energy in the C—— affair, suddenly came to a dead lock. I could not even get a letter from him, though I had never had but four, and after *pretending* to be ill, though I ascertained he came to his business every day, and, sending Mr. COLE to hunt him up, who never could find him either in his office or at his own house, and after fooling me in this manner for thirteen months ! this new addition to the scoundrelocracy flatly refused to give me up my documents about this iniquitous swindle until I had paid him £60 for torturing my life out, and doing worse than nothing, as usual selling me to my ruffianly and dastardly husband. Mr. COLE said his demands were simply preposterous and absurd. How differently would a French *juris consulte* have acted had the com-

monest woman in the place been so used by an *Avoué*, to whom
he had recommended her; he would very soon have brought him
to book, or have held him up to public scorn. But trust an
English barrister risking a single brief by embroiling himself
with any attorney if all the women in England had been skinned
by them to save parchment. Mr. COLE no doubt thought he was
doing great things in getting me Mr. COMYN of Lincoln's Inn,
his own solicitor (whose bill I had of course to pay), to cut down
that other bird of prey's extortion to £35, and at length got me
back my papers, when time, and COCKBURN, had given security
and consolidation to that meanest of all ruffians, Sir EDWARD
BULWER LYTTON, and as Mr. COLE refused a fee (as well he
might), I gave him a piece of plate that cost me £20, for the Englishman is not yet born whom I like sufficiently, or think sufficiently
well of, to rest under the cold shadow of an obligation to.

And here, as I am on COCKBURN, let me mention a curious
fact, which proves the sincerity of that intimacy and friendship
which existed between himself and Sir LIAR. I was one day
sitting in the breakfast-room, when ALEXANDER the Little was
suddenly shown in. Poor small man, how shabby, and how
frightened he looked! With tears in his eyes, he said that he
had been hunted about by bailiffs (or duns, I forget which) all
the morning; and had taken refuge here. He said he had not
been to chambers for several days, as he knew he should be
arrested; and having not a sou in his pockets, even to buy him
a dinner, he had called on my husband, as an old Cambridge
friend, to ask him for the loan of only five pounds. And the
poor dwarf looked haggard and hungry; and the tears were in
my eyes as I saw his woe-begone and famished face. I told him
my husband was in the next room, and that I had no doubt
when he heard the facts he would be happy to oblige him; and
I left C. in the breakfast-room, having ordered some coffee and
rolls for him, for I really thought he was starving. I then made
my way to Sir LIAR, and asked him for the cash. Oh! what a
scene! Sir LIAR swore like a trooper. He cursed, he raved, he
foamed at the mouth; for it seems he had been previously " not
at home " to his small friend, who had then, in despair, enquired
for me, and been shown in. His oaths, his fury were fearful.
He stamped about, raved like a madman, calling COCKBURN every
name of cheat, card-sharper, swindler, scoundrel, adulterer,
&c., &c. He poured forth all the choicest phrases of the
Dictionary of the Vulgar Tongue, which—I forget the fool's name
—one somebody has published. At length I was pushed
violently out of the room, and I came back to COCKBURN, who
by this time had devoured the rolls and swallowed the coffee. I
told him how sorry I was, that I could do nothing with Sir E.,
and, as I had no money of my own, I actually gave him a ring

off my finger for his necessities ; and he went down on his knees
and thanked me in the most abject manner that ever I saw in
my life.

But to come back to "Very Successful." Were you here
I could soon explain to you, *viva voce*, Sir LIAR'S *double*
motive in his conspiracy about this copyright, which does
not in any way appear on the *surface*, since in addition to his
usual efforts to crush *all* my books by the venal and unscrupulous
abuse of his literary gang, and so starve me out that way, he
took especial means to crush and defame that particular book
on its first appearance. But exclusive of the tax upon your time
and patience—having already written so much, and having still
so much to write, I can neither afford the time nor the space to
do so. And now for the Quaker Upholsterer and his £5 ! He
wrote letters innumerable to Dr. R—— about it (for after the
mean and barefaced lies of the latter in the plot, and about Mr.
IRONSIDE'S letters, I of course returned him his *Normandy presents*,
and renounced all further intercourse with him). OILY GAMMON
began by assuring FODEN LAWRENCE, the Quaker, that of *course*
he ought to be paid, and he *should* be paid. But, as usual,
the vane did not long remain towards one point. So at
last he wrote to say, he could not possibly recover the debt, not
having it included in the schedule of the other Taunton tradespeople's claims. I then of course offered to pay it to the poor
man. "No," said he, "not if thee were made of gold and swim-
ming in diamonds; I'll make them pay me and they shall." He
then wrote to Sir LIAR, who sent him back a demented looking
scrawl, which looked as if an insane spider had tumbled into the
ink, and then the webs of Sir L's. lies, being too flimsy to make it
a straight waistcoat, it had with *my* complaint ! *delirium tremens !*—
from the ink it had imbibed—frantically dashed itself against
the paper ; the purport of its plungings being to inform the
Quaker "that I had a most liberal (very ! !) allowance to pay
my own debts, and that Sir LIAR was neither morally nor legally
obliged to do so." The Quaker then wrote to E—— J—— a
few *highly spiced* truths about the infamy of the Madhouse Conspiracy (for you must know that friend LAWRENCE, albeit a man
of peace, was one of the most bellicose and irate of my many
indignant champions here) and more particularly of himself and
his client ! Whereupon EDWIN the Unfair wrote back that
neither he, nor Sir EDWARD BULWER LYTTON, were persons to be
bullied into anything.—" Well then," said the Quaker, making
his *debut* as a wit, on reading this letter to me, with an expression of face (as he held the letter at arm's length in one hand,
and shook the fingers of his other at it), the inimitable comi-
cality of which would have made the fortune of WEBSTER or
SAVASSEUR, " If *bullying* won't do, I'll try *courting* you—you pre-

cious pair!"—and he accordingly forthwith cited Sir LIAR to appear before the County Court, at which, by return of post, on the Sunday, so that LAWRENCE got it on the Monday, a cheque for the £5 was enclosed! but J——s dying hard—as he had lived—saying with a flourish on the last trumpet—" That although neither he nor Sir EDWARD LYTTON were either legally or morally bound to pay that £5, Sir EDWARD with his usual (ahem) generosity (!!!!), rather than Mr. LAWRENCE should be a loser, sent it!" The Quaker threw up his eyes piously, and said he hoped he should never want food or raiment till Sir EDWARD BULWER LYTTON was generous! or E—— J——s!!! and then sat down and wrote the Q.C. the following letter, of which I took a copy:—
"I have to acknowledge the receipt of the £5 due to me by Sir EDWARD BULWER LYTTON, which he and thee should have sent long ago, without putting me to the trouble of County Courting him. If, as he says, he is neither legally nor morally obliged to pay it; I am very *sure* it was both *legally* and *morally due to me;* or I neither should have demanded it, nor compelled thee and thy client to pay it.—FODEN LAWRENCE."

What I would give to have seen Sir LIAR's face when he read what the spirit, and a very proper spirit too, had moved the Quaker to write to him! No wonder that GOD's judgment overtook him, and that soon after, being more mad and outrageous than usual, the great man (very) was packed off to Algiers with two keepers. " *Vengeance is Mine, saith the Lord, I will repay.*"

It would appear that E—— J——, not having told lies enough, and done dirty work enough in the country, must needs re-commence after his outlawry; for it is only last year, in America, that upon a woman being tried for the murder of her husband, and the defence set up being his barbarous usage of her, that the Judge said, " If brutal usage and persecution was an excuse for committing murder, *I* ought to have murdered Sir EDWARD BULWER LYTTON long ago, if only *half* the papers had stated about his brutal treatment and persecutions of me was true." Whereupon, that model of all honour and truth! Mr. E—— J——, rose up in Court and said, " He must beg to set the Judge right on that point, for that Lady LYTTON had never complained (!!) of unkindness from Sir EDWARD, and *could* not!!! and that it was only last year, just before he (E—— J——) quitted England, that Sir EDWARD, having been left a large fortune by a relation" (Oh!! Mr. J——! what next? and next?) "he had *generously* doubled his wife's income"!!!!! There! let his Satanic Majesty beat *that* if he can! I of course instantly wrote to the *New York Times* (as these most infamous and barefaced lies had appeared in that beastly *Daily Telegraph*), refuting them, and saying, " that for the many colossal falsehoods, for which Mr. E——-J—— was proverbial, never had he dared to utter

ROBERT, LORD LYTTON.

any equal in magnitude to these! But as my doing so had of course been anticipated, and the Press of all countries is equally corrupt and venal, " *The Editor of the New York Times could not publish my letter, as its contents referred to strictly private and family matters!!* " This is quite England over again, where the most horrible lies and calumnies by a husband (in power) are to be given full and world-wide publicity! but if the victim wife dares to refute them, ah! *then* they become strictly private, and personal affairs, and *no* newspaper, for fear of the Law of Libel, will give any refutations admission into their columns! And so this meanest and cruellest of all Villains and Cowards! Sir EDWARD BULWER LYTTON, who has not even the courage of his loathsome vices, goes on for ever, strutting over the ruins of the moral Carthage *he* has razed, and heralding forth to posterity, through the brazen trumpet of mendacity, all the inverse virtues of his hideous and manifold vices. But let the wretch beware! The last time, a wave of my fan drove the cowardly reptile from the Hertford hustings, but only let him *dare* ever again to parade his physical and moral leprosy upon any hustings; and he shall find his escape shall not be so *easy*. After I had declined any further intercourse with my *useful*, and honourable, and veracious trustee, Dr. R——, his petty spite was to keep me each quarter two or three weeks out of my beggarly pittance, a most *serious* inconvenience to me; but their calculation was, no doubt, that I should, as of old, eat it all up in paying lawyers to obtain it, *Pas si bete*. So, pondering the matter a little while, a bright thought struck me. I went down to FODEN LAWRENCE the Quaker, and asked him "if he would each quarter, *on the day it was due*, pay me this beggarly £125, and send Dr. R—— my receipt for it, making him repay him. He said " with pleasure," and wrote to Dr. R—— : " As I think it a most scandalous shame that, used as she has already been, Lady LYTTON should be kept one hour out of so scandalously inadequate a pittance, I have this day paid her the £125 due to her; and *shall continue to do so punctually*, every quarter when it becomes due, and I enclose thee her receipt for the £125 paid this day, and will thank thee to send me a cheque by *return of post* for the amount.—FODEN LAWRENCE."

And as, like all knaves, these cowardly wretches are mortally afraid of an honest, straightforward, and *resolute* man, and of my fighting Quaker in particular, he has ever since, now four years, paid me to the day, and got the money from them by return of post. Meanwhile that dastardly villain, Sir EDWARD BULWER LYTTON, is comfortably playing out his game of lies; his victim buried alive, too poor to mix in the society to which she belongs, and too proud to go upon sponging visits she cannot repay by invitations in return, to say nothing of *this* being the *only* place I could ever feel *safe* in while that monster lives, as *here*, after the uproar there was, he never dare attempt any fresh villainy. I am doubly crippled by that trapped journey abroad, having done much, which having known all I *now* know, I should *not* have done. I don't mean about poor little JEANNE HESTIER, for that is a drop in the sea, and, morever, having told good Mrs. CLARKE that as long as I live, whether here or not, I shall always pay her the same, which I thought was the least I could do after her kindness and fidelity to me, you may suppose I have no money to go about with ; so being all the same as if I were buried dead, instead of only being buried alive, of course the outer public believe (as Sir LIAR has worked *so* hard for them to do) that I *really am* mad, or imbecile, or something, or else I of *course* should have brought an action for false imprisonment and conspiracy against those villainous mad doctors long ago, or got a divorce from that monster, or been seen or heard of somewhere. It is little matter what they think—GOD and my own conscience know the truth. But it is hard, bitterly cruelly hard! Still I would not change with one of the wretches, more especially H—— H——, and H——, who have now gone to their fearful account! A lady was here the other day, furious ! at that vile wretch, Sir L., having dared to come so near me as Bath. " Pooh.! never mind," said I, " He can't be more near than he has always been." About six months after my return from that trapped journey, I heard that Mr. ROBERT LYTTON'S marriage was broken off, his father having broken faith with him (as I told him he would), and given him nothing to marry on ; and that he had quarrelled with his father. He was then first paid *attaché* at Vienna ; despite my having written to him to say all intercourse must cease between us, when he was trying with that vile Miss R—— to purloin those letters ; now that he was in such deep misery, and I know in such deep humiliation, at the unworthy part he had acted when so noble a one was before him, I felt I was still his mother ; and wrote to him a letter, which, if he had had a heart of stone, provided it were only in the shape of a heart ! and a conscience, even if no bigger than a midje's egg, he would have answered ! but he never has. I then thought that if he could not trust the Embassy bag, and was equally afraid of the post with such a father, whose Jesuitical influence he believes to be ubiquitous— that as he was at Copenhagen when his great friend Sir AUGUSTUS PAGET came over here for the Prince of Wales's marriage, that surely he might have trusted him ;—but no —nothing. Never mind, he'll want me, before I want.

And now, sir, I ought to, and would make you many apologies for inflicting upon you such a long, and to you—necessarily uninteresting history—but that I read and *believed* the " Notice " appended to your last (*every* one says) "masterly work," and have done you the honour of taking you for an honest man. And hence this otherwise unwarrantable infliction. As I told you at the commencement of this letter, I want you to do nothing for me; for nothing *can* now be done; and yet for three things in your power to do, without in any way compromising yourself, I should be *very* grateful to you :—

Firstly. To *tell* the facts herein contained as far, and as wide as you can.

Secondly. In telling them, to say nothing of, or *nothing against* my truly unfortunate son, who, GOD knows, is *well* punished! for the fearful weakness in which he has been *purposely* trained, by his relentless and unscrupulous father, that he *might* effectually crush by moulding him resistlessly to his will.

Thirdly. As a man of real genius, as you are, you must be in the habit of analysing human nature, by a sort of psychological vivisection, or you never could produce the photographs of characters you do. Can you then conjecture, or suggest any clue, to my unhappy son's contradictory conduct? Emanating as it were from two distinctly *opposite natures;* the one almost angelic, the other almost the reverse. But putting his weakness, and more than Hamletish *dreamy irresolution* out of the analysis; you must not seek a solution of his unworthy conduct in the equally unworthy and mundane fear of being disinherited. No doubt his vile father! *would* leave him a beggar, if he could, but that he might not immolate all to his own Juggernaut selfishness, Knebworth is not only strictly entailed upon his son, but luckily, stringently 12 deep after him, or Sir L. might have got his poor weak victim to cut off the entail. If you can solve this enigma, I should be so grateful.

I have the honour to be, sir,

Your obedient servant,

ROSINA BULWER LYTTON.

Wednesday, February 10th, 1864.

P.S.—One thing I forgot to mention to you, which was, that the last time I saw that double-dealing sneak, Dr. R——, which was the day that upon leaving town I asked him to write to Mr. IRONSIDE about the swindle of my book; he said suddenly, *apropos de bottes,* "the fact is we have been *completely sold!*" which solitary truth from him was, as you may suppose, a great consolation to me, seeing how indefatigably *he* had assisted in selling me. He then added, clenching his hand, and muttering to himself "Well, I think I'd have begged my bread before I could have used *my* mother so!" It is *he* that would! But it is *so* easy always to *say* the right and *do* the wrong thing, which is the compromise most men make with the Devil.—R.B.L.

Appendix.

ALL my Lord LYTTON's infamy, and my fame as a patient Grizzle was pretty well established—and even acknowledged by the wretch who benefitted by it—for one day at a dinner at our house, when some vituperative humbug was going on about poor Lord BYRON, and someone said, " No woman could have lived with such a man," my Lord LYTTON pointed to me, and said, " There is one that could, for she has lived with me." And in that letter he wrote about his going abroad and changing his name (why the—Lady SYKES didn't he)—all of which is from beginning to end as usual—after biting my cheek, though of course he began it with a well-studied colossal lie about the "visible restraint he had tried to put upon himself, and his doubting whether it was humane to goad a man with his terrible infirmity (to wit, a diabolical and unbridled temper), but being himself to blame, God forbid he should judge others." Sweet, patient, virtuous, just creature! Now the goading and provocation I had given him was this. Having asked him before dinner for a little money to pay some of the housebills left owing before we went to Italy—where he had so beggared himself *on himself* buying statues, &c., &c., that he had to retrench in every way upon me and the children, and began by taking away my carriage horses —and I had been ordered to stand sponsor to that vulgar Mrs. FONBLANQUE's child, I had to ask Lady STEPNEY to take me! He said at dinner, How are you going to FONBLANQUE's to night? I told him, whereupon he began with a sardonic grin, and repeating a dozen times, humming, " My mother calls Lady STEPNEY that ugly old woman." I made no reply, when he thundered out, " Do you hear me, madame?" "Yes, of course I hear you." " Then why the d——l in h—ll " (which being *his* strong language, of course that concrete ass, the British public, would consider as fine writing!) " Then why the d——l in h—ll don't you answer me ?" " I did not consider it required an answer." Whereupon he rose, seizing a carving knife, and crying as he darted at me, " D——n your soul, madam, I'll have you to know that whenever *I* do you the honour of addressing you it requires an answer." Seeing the glitter of the knife, I cried out "For GOD's sake, EDWARD, take care of what you are about," at which he dropped the knife, and springing on me like a tiger, made his hideous teeth meet in my left cheek. My screams brought the servants back into the room, one of whom tried to collar him, but he broke from him, and putting on one of the footmen's hats! rushed down Piccadilly, and from thence betook himself to Richmond, from whence four days after he wrote me that letter, which from being read and re-read is in too worn a state to be trusted to the casualties of the Post. Well, in *that* letter, occurs the following paragraph *underlined*, " You have for the last six years " (the whole time of our marriage), " *been to me an incomparable wife*, and if for the last year, you have judged my character too harshly," &c., &c., &c , &c., &c. Now this too harsh judgment here alluded to rose from a mere trifle, which of course a " ladylike," feminine, lachrymose, clever woman carrying on her *own* game, would have thought nothing of. He had been intriguing with a Mrs. ROBERT STANHOPE, and exhibiting himself and her in every drawing-room. But it was not I, patient Grizzle, who made the scandal about it—but her husband's relations—Lady TAVISTOCK at the head, whereupon that charming man gave me his solemn oath (his! or his son's cath !!) that everything was at an end between them, and went on his knees to me, to go to Italy with him. When I did so, the vessel had not sailed an hour, when who should I see but Mrs. ROBERT STANHOPE sitting wrapped up—my Lord LYTTON at her feet, and her contemptible little wretch of a husband (who my Lord LYT-TON afterwards told me used to sell her to men*) looking on. Nor was this enough—I was forced by brutal threats, and per-sonal violence—to offer this woman a seat in my carriage to Paris —and the brutality I endured there—it would take reams of paper to describe. Oh ! oh ! oh ! cries manly, and " ladylike " conventionality. " You should have returned to England, in-stantly from Calais." " Very true, my dear madam, there was only one little, but still *insurmountable* impediment, viz., the same which at this moment prevents my leaving Taunton, and freeing myself from one of the cruel and degrading tortures I am endur-ing, and which are so truly, though, alas ! so slowly killing me— that all-powerful one of not having a shilling ! Many years ago —two or three after it was written, I showed that cheek-biting letter to Dr. LUSHINGTON, who was, of course, too busy to give a pauper anything but the English parish order of verbal sym-pathy ; but never so long as I live shall I forget the probing, searching, expression of those keen analytic eyes of his, as look-ing up from the very first page of that letter, he said, " This man has been in the habit of ill-using you ? " " What makes you think so ? " said I. " Two circumstances. First, the great and palpably artful pains he takes to convey the idea—knowing, of

---

* This is something like RICHARDSON'S transfer to HOLKER ; and HOLKER'S anticipated assignment to MONTAGU CORRY : and HOLKER like COPLEY, or LYNDHURST, will no doubt sit on the Bench !!! Thus HOLKER helps to get Dr. KENEALY disbarred and destroyed, because, unlike HOLKER, he is not fit to belong to an " honourable profession," and all the Ministry look on, and uphold, and applaud ! !!

course, such a letter would be read—that he put every possible restraint upon himself, as—if you had been exasperating him—he proves rather too much there. The second is : the equally artful pains he takes to talk of this outrage, as a first and *solitary* one ! Now, *no* man ever got to such a pitch of brutality at a *first* essay." And yet, what was all this, compared to his perversion of the only child his brutality had left me—oh ! the black, fiendish cruelty of it ! As this great genius (?) has nothing original about him but his sin, and therefore must always plagiarise from some-one, I can fancy him giving his instructions to his son, and when I was entrapped abroad in 1858, saying to him, with a sardonic grin, which it is to be hoped his worthy pupil reflected—as he borrowed ISAAC WALTON'S receipt for impaling a wretched frog—only substituting her for him, " Use her as though you loved her !" And so the hook was baited with my own heart.

An astute, unscrupulous Villain, who from the hour I was turned out of my house, has been working *systematically* to starve me out by *never* having given me enough to live on ! He *premeditated this* before we married, when then not having an acre of land in the world—(for it was my little pittance of £350 a year that gave him a qualification for Parliament), he settled the munificent sum of £1,030 on me to *bar dower.* Soon his necessity made him want what little land I had, and though strictly tied upon me, I gave it up,—the sole surviving trustee to my marriage settlement being *then* his brother WILLIAM BULWER. Soon after this he again wanted money. I said, You know I have no more,—" Yes, you have that £1,000 I settled upon you to bar dower." Oh ! I said that is neither worth giving or refusing. Now this reminds me to answer your other questions. The sum my Lord LYTTON paid for my 25 years' debts, to patch up the Madhouse conspiracy, was £3,500, and Mr. HYDE told me, and I think he also wrote it in one of his letters while I was abroad: " Sir EDWARD boasts that he has generously given you back all your own money, to pay your debts; and I'm sure you would rather feel this than be beholden to him."

Supplemental Notes.

THE CASE OF LADY BULWER LYTTON.

From the *Somerset County Gazette and West of England Advertiser*,
July 13th, 1858.

FOR some three years past a lady, rather above middle age,
of somewhat portly figure and handsome countenance, has
occupied apartments in the quiet, comfortable, and pleasant
establishment at Taunton, known as CLARKE'S Hotel. Her
appearance, manners, and habits, so far as the latter were known,
did not cause her to be particularly noticed as she walked in
public; for she was much like ordinary ladies—plainly and
becomingly dressed—conducted herself with propriety, remarked
objects that were likely to attract attention, and passed without
notice those that were not so. She sometimes did a little "shop-
ping," as ladies generally are fond of doing, and when she asked
for any particular article, she did so in ordinary terms, and
answered questions in a rational manner, though at times with
haughtiness. In her country walks she was occasionally accompanied by a female friend, though generally in these her only
companion was a little dog, for which she always showed great
fondness. Sometimes also she has been seen at public enter-
tainments, though but seldom, and there her attire has been
similarly becoming to that in her walks in town or country. In
a place like Taunton, a person of any note does not long reside
before he or she becomes known to many of the inhabitants; and
soon after the arrival of the lady we have been describing she
was generally known to be Lady BULWER LYTTON, wife of the
eminent novelist, who now holds the distinguished position of
Colonial Secretary in her Majesty's Government.

Persons who are in a state of madness give indications of their
misfortunes at home and abroad. They

> " Bend their eyes on vacancy,
> And with the incorporeal air do hold discourse;
> Their words are loose
> As heaps of sand, and scattering wide from sense; "

But Lady LYTTON during the three years she was at Taunton
never did aught that we are aware of (and we have taken pains
to ascertain the truth) to cause in any one with whom she had
communication the slightest suspicion that in her case reason
had been dethroned, or that her brain was in any degree affected
with lunacy. Yet this lady has been taken from the quiet re-

treat she had chosen in this fair town of Somerset—perhaps we might say to which she was driven—and carried to one of those miserable abodes of the most hapless of human beings—a "Madhouse."

The circumstances under which Taunton has lost one of its inhabitants, are so extraordinary and so shocking, that, as may be supposed, they have greatly excited the minds of the people generally. Upon those persons who were on terms of intimacy with Lady LYTTON (they were only few, for she evinced little inclination to mix in society, and it was pretty well known that her pecuniary means were too limited to allow of her doing so), upon her personal friends the first mention of the fact fell like a clap of thunder, when the skies give no sign of an approaching storm. They could not credit such strange information with truth; but when convinced of its veracity their exclamation has been, "Good Heavens! Lady LYTTON in a *Madhouse*. For what? Who can have sent her there? She is no more mad than I am, or any one else." And those who have merely seen her as she passed them in the streets or other public highways, have been hardly less startled by the intelligence. There is on all hands a firm belief that this unfortunate lady—we say unfortunate in allusion only to her present lamentable position, and without reference to circumstances which have given both to herself and her husband an unenviable notoriety—there is, we say, a firm belief that Lady LYTTON is the subject of a horrible and appalling injustice and wrong; that while perfectly sane she has been shut up in a lunatic asylum, merely in order that a woman who has, no doubt, been a constant source of annoyance to her husband, may be prevented for ever, from again giving him similar trouble, or again molesting him in any way. In ascribing to her the character we have given, we desire to avoid the indication of any opinion as to her conduct towards Sir EDWARD, or as to his general treatment of her. We only state a fact, that people among whom she has resided during a period of three years—to many of whom she is well and intimately known, and most of whom have had frequent opportunities of seeing her—believe that though sent to an asylum for lunatics, her intellect is perfectly sound, and therefore that she has been made, for some reason or other, the victim of an atrocity which a hundred years ago might have excited no great attention beyond the circle of the doomed one's own relatives, but which cannot be overlooked in the present age without danger to "that liberty of the subject" which has been since achieved, and which is the highest boast and most glorious privilege of the people of this country.

In giving to Lady LYTTON the character we have ascribed, and in stating what is the general opinion of her in this town, we by no means wish to have it supposed that we regard her as one of the most pleasant or amiable of women. Her later literary works (for none of which can be claimed any considerable praise) seem to have been undertaken in a great measure for the purpose of publishing to the world her own sufferings, and of exposing what she conceived to be the foul treatment she received from one who vowed at the altar to " love and cherish her "; and in more than one instance her writings evince unkind and uncharitable feelings towards very estimable and excellent persons. We particularly allude to one of her latest productions, entitled, "Very Successful," in which a lady of this town, who is only known to be respected and esteemed, is held up to most undeserved ridicule for no other reason than that she did not desire to cultivate her ladyship's acquaintance, having, probably from the nature of her daily engagements, little time to give to the maintenance of friendships beyond the circle of associates she had already gathered around her. And we happen to know that in several cases her ladyship has manifested much haughtiness to persons who have had occasion to come in contact with her. But such things as these, however much to be deprecated in all persons, certainly cannot be regarded as evidence of a deranged brain, for if unkind and offensive personalities in print were so considered, few writers would be safe from incarceration in a Lunatic Asylum; and if haughtiness were held to be a proof of lunacy, who is there that should give the necessary " certificates," and who become " warders "? Displays of ill-temper and malignity, of pride and arrogance, are never very reasonable; they are in truth very ridiculous; still there is much yet to be learnt if they are to be held as indications of madness. We make these remarks to show that, while under an impression—we will say a conviction—that in Lady LYTTON's transfer to a Lunatic Asylum she has been made the victim of a shocking outrage and crime, we are not unacquainted with, or insensible to, her weaknesses and defects. And we may here state that our object in alluding to her case at all is to enforce by its publicity that strict investigation into its circumstances to which she is in common justice entitled, and which society demands for its own satisfaction and as its own safeguard.

Lady LYTTON when married, in 1827, to Sir EDWARD, possessed a small property worth about £400 per annum, and it is stated that, her husband being then in far less affluent circumstances than at present, she transferred this to him, in order to give him a qualification for a seat in Parliament. Her experience of the married state was an unhappy one, and in 1838 a separation took place by mutual consent, Sir EDWARD consenting to pay her £400 a year during his life, which has been her allowance from that to the present time, notwithstanding he is, or is reputed to be, a

G

wealthy man, his annual income being estimated at from £8,000 to £10,000.

Four hundred a-year being unequal to the requirements of a lady who had moved in the higher classes of society—leaving luxuries out of the question—Lady LYTTON became involved in debt, which of late has claimed about one half of her income, and of course every year saw her sink deeper and deeper into the mire. One of her chief complaints against her husband was, the smallness of the means he allowed her for her support, and certainly if, as is stated, his own income is £10,000, it is a very reasonable one—for the allowance of £8 a year to his wife by a man whose income is £200 would be just in the same proportion; and there are few who would not decry and condemn the injustice which such a payment by a person having £200 a-year would exhibit. By the deed of separation Lady LYTTON was to possess in her own right any property she might acquire thereafter, which has been chiefly from her publications—in some cases remunerative, but in others miserable failures. She has been severely censured for the bitterness displa-ed in some of her writings, but perhaps not altogether with justice. Let those who would condemn the use of harsh language just learn under what circumstances it has been used; and if they find the author's life has been one of excessive trial and suffering—that she has either been compelled to quit, or has felt it imperatively necessary to flee from, the house of her husband—that from a position of pecuniary ease she has been cast down to a condition of humiliating poverty—that instead of her society being courted by numerous "friends" whose acts of kindness caused her days to pass lightly and happily, she is shunned by most of them as no longer worthy of their regard—that while her husband still moves among the gayest and noblest of society, she remains the occupant of two small rooms in a country hotel—if they make in her case the allowance which such an accumulation of woes and miseries ought to ensure, they will not fail to be very sparing of censure—they will hardly express surprise, perhaps, at the display of ill-feeling, however bitter or general it may be. When a person is treated as an Ishmael, it is not to be wondered at if he regards himself as such; and the test of tempers will at last be soured and ruined by constant irritation and suffering. A not very high authority has said, "Revenge is sweet, especially to women." Perhaps he did not flatter the sex when he so wrote; but assuredly if there are ever circumstances in which the worm will turn, and may be pardoned for turning, they are such as are here represented. It is human so to turn, as it is to "err" generally. When persons are under a higher influence than any which belongs to mere humanity, they may adopt a higher line of conduct, and submit patiently to whatever befalls them, under a conviction that it is good for them to suffer; but Lady LYTTON has never made any pretensions or professions that would justify the higher standard to her case, and therefore should not be too hardly judged. Divesting one's thoughts of the unfavourable effect produced by her display of bitter feeling towards others—though they are those to whom she ascribes treatment almost too dreadful for human endurance—her life appears unsullied and blameless. This is a tribute undeniably her due.

Lady LYTTON has for some years past endeavoured to obtain an increase to her allowance, which in consequence of the liabilities which she had incurred and was obliged to meet as best she could, had fallen to about £180 per annum; but her appeals, is not wholly disregarded, were quite unsuccessful. Continually smarting under the denial of her claims, and rendered desperate probably by increasing difficulties, she determined to adopt a step which might prove more effective in this behalf than the means she had previously employed. Sir EDWARD having recently accepted office as a Cabinet Minister, the seat he held in Parliament as one of the members for Hertfordshire became vacant, and according to custom it was necessary for him to meet his constituents in order to his re-election. Lady LYTTON resolved to be present upon that occasion, and to take a conspicuous part in the proceedings. Before she left Taunton she caused handbills to be circulated in Hertfordshire in which it was announced that she would address the assembled electors on the day of the nomination; and accompanied by a female friend, she proceeded by railway to Oxford, and thence posted to Hertford. Precaution seems to have been taken to prevent the scandal which had been thus threatened, and on her arriving at the hotel, and asking at what hour the proceedings at the hustings would commence, she was answered that it was twelve o'clock— the fact being that eleven was the time appointed. Shortly before twelve, still in the company of her friend, she drove to the hustings in a hired carriage, and arrived there just in time to hear her husband close his address with an eloquent tribute to the galaxy of beauty by which he was surrounded. The scene that followed is thus graphically described in a London contemporary:—

"Towards the close of the proceedings of the Hertfordshire election, just after Sir EDWARD had concluded his address with a fervent tribute of admiration to the womanly beauty exhibited in the long line of open carriages, chaises and vans, drawn up in front of the hustings, there was an unwonted stir in the crowd, which parted to admit of the passage of a hired brougham from one of the town inns. Two ladies alighted—one an exceedingly

G 2

handsome woman of about 45 years of age, with fresh complexion and eyes of dazzling beauty. Evidently labouring under excitement, she advanced through the crowd towards the hustings, and announced herself as the wife of Sir E. BULWER LYTTON. She had come according to promise to confront her husband and expose the wrongs described in her works and in a pamphlet. The appearance of the lady was not unexpected, as her coming had been announced in placards and bills; but some person had detained her while the election was proceeding in the vicinity. Recognised, as soon as observed, her voice was nearly drowned by the shouts of Sir EDWARD'S supporters : but Sir EDWARD'S eye caught hers, and his face paled. He looked like a man suddenly attacked by paralysis. Those near him say he trembled exceedingly. For a few moments he retained his position in front of the hustings, and turned his back on the unwelcome visitor. Then he suddenly disappeared below the hustings platform, while his wife cried 'COWARD,' and he having hastily signed the usual declaration, escaped into the residence of the gentleman on whose grounds the election took place. Lady LYTTON continued to address the audience assembled for more than a quarter of an hour. Her ladyship subsequently made an application to the Mayor for the use of the Town Hall, for the purpose of making a public statement; but this being refused her, she left the town early in the afternoon. Lady LYTTON arrived in Hertford at three o'clock on the morning of the election, having posted from Taunton, where she resides. It is needless to say that the event has caused the greatest possible excitement in Hertfordshire."

For several months past, her ladyship was under an impression that she was closely watched, and she seemed to be suspicious that the object of this espionage was the miserable fate which has at last fallen upon her.

Circumstances occurred about a month ago that were of a character to confirm her apprehensions. At that time a gentleman came to Taunton, and took up his residence at the Castle Hotel, which was in close contiguity to the house in which she resided. He had had a great deal to do with the subject of her separation from Sir EDWARD, being, in fact, the honourable baronet's solicitor, and she held him in extreme aversion. He remained here some short time, it is said, and then left, but not before his sojourn had become known to her ladyship. On the 12th of June, another gentleman arrived in Taunton, and calling at CLARKE'S Hotel, sent his card to Lady LYTTON, with a request for an interview. This was a "Dr. THOMPSON," and he was accompanied by a nurse from a neighbouring lunatic asylum. After some reflection, her ladyship consented to his admission, but took the precaution to request the landlady's presence during his stay. Mrs. CLARKE was present accordingly, and we are informed that the conversation which ensued between Lady LYTTON and Dr. THOMPSON, originated and sustained by him, referred wholly to subjects that were calculated to excite intense anger and indignation on her part. This interview lasted five hours, and at last she asked if he had not come from Mr. LOADER, Sir EDWARD'S solicitor, to which interrogatory he answered, " I am." Her ladyship, who had preserved unwonted calmness, then asked, " Is the farce played out?—and if not, how much longer is it to last?" Dr. THOMPSON replied, "The farce is ended. and your ladyship will not, from this hour, hear any more upon these painful matters." It may be stated that during the interview, two police officers, a solicitor, and a medical gentleman, were in the adjoining room, the object of whose presence it is not difficult to imagine. But Lady LYTTON'S calmness rendered their presence unnecessary. Previous to his departure, Dr. THOMPSON requested her to put upon paper what demand she wished to make upon her husband; and she complied, writing in substance as follows:—"Sir EDWARD to pay my debts, the interest of which swallows up the greater part of my income, and increase my income to £500 a year. Upon his doing this, I solemnly promise never again to molest him in any way, nor even to mention his name." Dr. THOMPSON premised to lay these requirements before Sir EDWARD immediately upon his return to London, and then withdrew, Lady LYTTON giving vent on his departure to her overwrought feelings in a flood of tears, which could not be restrained for a considerable time, notwithstanding the consolation offered by the landlady, whose kindness to her throughout these painful and sad proceedings had been very great; and even of the nurse, whose opinion as to the state of her ladyship's mind had undergone a considerable change since the time she was in her presence.

Several days elapsed, and still no communication arriving from Dr. THOMPSON, Lady LYTTON naturally became impatient, and she wrote him, reminding him of his promise, and requesting information as to his success with Sir EDWARD. No answer was received to her letter, and she addressed him again and again with the same result. Unable to remain longer in suspense, upon a matter of such moment, she at last wrote to him to the effect that she would go to London in the course of the following week, and hoped to be able to see him with a view to a final arrangement. Unfortunately for her, she carried out her intention.

Accompanied by a Miss RYVES, and a lady of Taunton, who has always taken an interest in her affairs, and will hereafter be found, it is presumed, capable of rendering her very important service in the proceedings which are contemplated, with a view to prove her sanity, Lady LYTTON took an evening train, and arrived in London shortly after 5 o'clock in the morning, a dreary time to enter the great lumbering city, even when one's business is of no such dreary character as theirs. The chief reason of their travelling by night instead of by day, was the inability of the female friend referred to, to remain away from her home more than one day. But another may have been a sudden desire of Lady LYTTON's to know, without further delay, what determination, if any, her husband had come to with respect to her written request, taken charge of by Dr. THOMPSON—an insatiable craving for the answer which should place her in comparatively pecuniary ease, or doom her still to the "shameful needs of poverty." Entering an hotel, they partook of refreshments, and whiled away, as well as they could, the lagging hours until what was deemed an appropriate time to call upon Dr. THOMPSON came round. They then s t out, and on reaching his house were courteously received. It was remarked by the doctor, however, that as they had come rather early, " Would they do him the favour to postpone discussion of the subject which had brought them until five o'clock in the afternoon?" Assent was, of course, given, and at the hour specified they were again at the door of his residence. On announcing their names, they were shown into the drawing-room, and Dr. THOMPSON waited upon them. He had hastily closed the door, however, when it was again opened, and another gentleman entered—"A friend of mine, who has casually dropped in." It was remarked that, notwithstanding the subject to be discussed, and which had been broached, was quite of a private nature, the friend kept his seat, and that though he took no part in the conversation, he listened attentively to what was said. There being signs that the interview was near its close, he withdrew. Lady LYTTON seemed to have, on entering the house, a presentiment that there was no favourable information for her, and after putting a few questions to Dr. THOMPSON, which he answered hesitatingly, she said, " You have not consulted Sir EDWARD, Dr. THOMPSON; tell me, is not that the case?" He owned that he could not give her any satisfactory answer, and her ladyship arose with her friends to depart, Dr. THOMPSON expressing a desire that she would not hurry away. Nevertheless she proceeded, and, on getting outside the room, was astonished to see before her two policemen, two women who had the appearance of nurses, and a gentleman who, it has since been found, is a keeper of a Lunatic Asylum in the neighbourhood of London. Dissemblance or concealment being no longer necessary or possible, the purpose of this assembly was in a few words explained.

There are not many persons in existence, mad or not mad, who on a discovery of so horrifying a nature would not have become wild with excitement, and fallen into a state closely bordering upon insanity; but Lady LYTTON sustained throughout these most trying and frightful circumstances a calm and dignified demeanour. She was indeed the calmest of the two—herself and her Taunton friend—for the affrighted Miss RYVES had rushed into the street. She was ushered into another room, on entering which she observed a figure, like that of Sir EDWARD'S, hastily retreating by a door at the other end. At first she refused to yield up her liberty, but the policemen were called, and she then said, "Resistance being vain, I submit, but under compulsion." Her friend insisted upon accompanying her, and she saw on the table in the room a paper which she presumed to be a certificate of Lady LYTTON'S insanity. Upon this were the names of two medical gentlemen, and it is believed of Sir EDWARD. Her lady-ship being requested to proceed to the door, where she was told a carriage was ready to receive her, again refused compliance except under compulsion; and on this the policemen, each taking an arm, led her forward—her friend—the only one she could in these tremendous moments of agony appeal to—endeavouring to console her and seeming to comfort her by the confident exclamations, "Never mind, Lady LYTTON; they may take you, but they cannot take me. You may be inside the Asylum, but I shall be out." One might suppose that under such circumstances some gentleman to whom her ladyship was known, some male friend, would have been requested to attend and witness proceedings which were so terribly to affect her, which were to convey her to a living tomb, to worse than death; but, besides the lady to whom we have so often referred, there was no one present on Lady LYTTON'S part. The policemen "did their duty," and her lady-ship was constrained to enter the carriage, her friend forcing herself in immediately after, and refusing to leave her. One or two gentlemen also seating themselves within it, the party was rapidly driven to an Asylum at Brentford, kept by a person of the name of HILL.

Arrived at the gates of the gloomy abode, the ladies were told they must part, and after a short scene, which we will not attempt to depict, they separated, the gates closing on "The Insane," and her friend being driven back to her lodgings. Previous to this lady's leaving London, she received a note from Sir EDWARD'S solicitor, in which it was stated that the hon. baronet would be glad to see her at his residence, No. 1, Park-lane. • She indignantly declined the interview. Shortly after-wards the solicitor called and represented that it might be ad-vantageous to her to see Sir EDWARD; but she gave him a denial in similar terms, and immediately returned to Taunton.

On the following day the Solicitor came to Taunton, and calling upon Mrs. CLARKE, demanded all the documents and other papers and such other property as Lady LYTTON had left; but Mrs. CLARKE refused to deliver and dared him to remove any of them, alleging as one reason that she had a lien upon them in the shape of a bill of £300 against her Ladyship; but in truth she was fortified in her refusal by a letter from Mr. HYDE, Lady LYTTON's solicitor, who had previously informed her, if any attempt should be made to take the property, or any part of it, she would be justified in calling in the police and giving the party into custody. Mr. LOADER offered to pay the bill, but the answer to this was, " I would rather forfeit every shilling of it than deliver the goods to you. They are in my possession, and I will not allow of their removal." Finding persuasion vain, Mr. LOADER retired.

We have said Lady LYTTON's capture, and the circumstances connected with it, have caused a great degree of excitement among the inhabitants of this town, and if any proof of this were called for, or any evidence of the opinion generally entertained required, we could hardly give more indubitable testimony than is contained in the following resolutions, which were adopted at a meeting of inhabitants called by a gentleman who, though a perfect stranger to Lady LYTTON, felt that a monstrous injustice had been inflicted upon her, and determined to use the very considerable influence he possessed to obtain her freedom if really not insane, or at least to force on such an inquiry into her mental condition as to satisfy the public that she is not in a fit state to be at liberty. The gentleman in question arrived in this town only a day or two before the case came to his knowledge, and immediately upon becoming acquainted with it he proceeded into the street, called together such of the more influential inhabitants as he met, and within an hour the meeting took place. After a discussion of the subject, the resolutions were thrown into the following form :—

"At a meeting of certain inhabitants of Taunton and the neighbourhood, held at Clarke's Hotel on the 6th of July, 1858. Mr. HITCHCOCK in the chair, it was resolved :—

"On the motion of Capt. JONES, seconded by R. EASTON, Esq.

" 1. That the removal of Lady BULWER LYTTON to a Lunatic Asylum, or other place of confinement, and the circumstances under which she was incarcerated therein, call for a public expression of alarm for the rights and liberties of the subject, and particularly of distrust of the treatment to which her ladyship is said to have been subjected.

" 2. That a Committee be now appointed to watch the result of the extraordinary measures reported to have been adopted in Lady LYTTON's case, to the end that the public mind may be satisfied, through their report, that in her ladyship's case justice may be done.—W. R. HITCHCOCK.

"The meeting was then adjourned for a week."

Here we will leave this miserable tale, but we are anxious, before closing our remarks, to avow that in taking it upon ourselves to set it before the public, we are actuated only by a sense of duty and justice. For the truth of the narrative, we can refer to the lady who accompanied Lady LYTTON to London; the details are given as they were furnished to us—without exaggeration or distortion. If her ladyship's mind is in such a state that she is a fit subject for a lunatic asylum, and an asylum is the only suitable place for her, no harm can come from the publicity we give to her case; if not, then much good must inevitably arise from its publicity, to her chiefly and in an immeasurable degree, but also to society in no unimportant measure. The whole question is, of course—Is Lady LYTTON actually insane? We have said, from what we have seen and heard of her, she is not; and this view is entertained by all we have heard express any opinion on the subject. It is a question of deep importance whether it is not utterly wrong, and most dangerous to the liberties of individuals, that upon the word of two medical men persons may be taken to a madhouse, when if not already insane, they are undoubtedly placed in circumstances in every way calculated, by their horrible and frightful character, to destroy reason and produce insanity. We say nothing of their continued confinement, but of their being consigned to such a place even for a moment. On every account a power of such awful magnitude should be destroyed, and confinement in a lunatic asylum be possible only after a public enquiry, similar to that which must precede the committal of a person accused of felony to the common gaol. Society in general demands this; helpless women require it; and if there are any individuals for the sake of whose character and reputation before the world the change should be made, they are those who occupy such a position as Sir EDWARD LYTTON now holds in her Majesty's Government. As a Secretary of State, he, as is well known, exercises great authority in such cases; and men so highly stationed can always find ready tools for any work, however nefarious. It is right then that suspicion against them should be rendered impossible, that no reasonable person should have ground for the supposition that they have committed or connived at an atrocity at which the body shudders and the mind is appalled. It is true that investigation into cases like that of Lady LYTTON is compelled when demanded by the friends of the incarcerated person; but the system is altogether contrary to the general equity of British laws and customs. To send to a madhouse a person suspected of lunacy, and afterwards institute an enquiry whether he is mad or not, is a mode of procedure very unworthy of a civilised nation, and which the people of this country ought no longer to endure. Lady

LYTTON'S case will no doubt have the effect of drawing general attention to this great anomaly, and probably it will tend in a great measure to the accomplishment of the desired change. Heaven grant it may be so!

THE CASE OF LADY LYTTON.

To the Editor of the Daily Telegraph.

SIR,—Can you inform me whether Mr. B. W. PROCTER, an intimate friend of Sir BULWER LYTTON, is a Commissioner of Lunacy? Can you also state whether Mr. JOHN FORSTER, also an intimate friend of Sir EDWARD, is Secretary to the Lunacy Commission?—Your obedient servant, DOUBTFUL. [Our correspondent is correct in assuming that Mr. PROCTER is a Lunacy Commissioner, and that the Secretary to the Commission is Mr. JOHN FORSTER.]

NOTE BY THE EDITOR.—This JOHN FORSTER was afterwards rewarded for his guilty complicity in this most horrible transaction by being made a Commissioner of Lunacy himself with a salary of £2,000 a year. He died very rich, no one knowing how his wealth was got. He was on the most social terms with three very wicked men—DICKENS, LYTTON, and COCKBURN.

Daily Telegraph, July 15th, 1858.

Sir EDWARD BULWER LYTTON has succeeded in hushing up the scandal of his wife's arrest and conveyance to a madhouse at Brentford. The matters in dispute, so say the persons interested, will be arranged to the satisfaction of all concerned. For the sake of the lady herself the public will rejoice that such a compromise has been extorted from the Secretary of State; if the victim be content no one has a right to complain, but it must be remembered that Sir BULWER LYTTON alone has gained by the suppression of enquiry. We are now told that he will seal a treaty of perpetual truce with the woman who was, apparently under his instruction, dragged by policemen into a carriage, hurried to a lunatic asylum, and there compelled to sign a compact of forbearance towards the individual by whom, according to her statement, she had been grossly and flagitiously wronged. It is with pleasure we record that this ignominious family war has been terminated, and the accusation of insanity has been abandoned; that Lady LYTTON is confessedly qualified to treat with her husband upon terms of equality. Justice may

boast of a triumph, for though it would have been more satisfactory to have forced the entire transaction before an authentic
tribunal, it may suffice to know that popular opinion has driven
Lord DERBY'S choice and brilliant colleague into a virtual sur-
render. It matters little whether Sir BULWER LYTTON, under
Cabinet influence, has found it necessary to save the reputation
of the government as well as his own, but it is not to be forgotten that he employed attorneys, nurses and policemen to
capture his wife; that she was forcibly consigned to a lunatic
asylum—that medical certificates were obtained to prove her insanity, and that now, an explosion of national feeling having
taken place, she is to be released and allowed to live in personal
independence.

All that now remains for investigation is who and what the
professional gentlemen were who handed over this lady to the
keepers of a madhouse; whether she was sane at the time of
her capture, and whether she was not kidnapped by the myrmidons of her flattered and successful husband. Individually
she may benefit by the compromise, though it may be that a
salutary exposure has been stifled. On one point the public are
agreed; the power at present exercised under the lunacy law of
England is dangerous to social liberty. Anyone, by obtaining
the certificate of two medical men, may imprison wife, child, or
other relative, for years, perhaps for life, in a madhouse. The
Lunacy Commissioners, we are reminded, may interfere with its
machinery of visitors' inspections and reports, but what is the
result? Men might be named who open establishments of this
character, accumulate fortunes, and live in affluence, and are
pointed at by their neighbours as the creatures of conspiracy.
Their residences are nobly furnished, their grounds rival those
of the nobility, and when official visitors, after sumptuous
luncheons, pass their patients in review, and an exasperated
captive pours forth his vehement denunciations, "they write
him down mad," and the wretch is left for another year, to be
goaded by a sense of wrong, wrought upon by the contagious
presence of insanity, and at length made all that his officious
friends desire him to be. Without casting a general slur upon a
body of men, many of whom are highly respectable, we may state
it as the conviction of those who stand above all prejudice in
their profession, that the lunatic asylums of this country are frequently applied to the same uses as the Bastille, where the Man
in the Iron Mask was immured for life and buried in secrecy
because his pretensions were considered dangerous by claimants
to estates and titles, or perpetrators of unsearched crimes.

But a social question of far more universal importance
is connected with the deplorable disclosure in the case of
Sir BULWER LYTTON. The baronet's wife may be released from

the terrible captivity to which, by the practical confession of her persecutors, she never ought to have been for a moment consigned, and from which we have made no unsuccessful effort to deliver her ; but what of humbler persons ? What of the domestic victims in whose name no publicity is invoked? We hear of jealous and bitter-tongued women, of outcast wives, who go down to bury their humiliation in the shade of equivocal watering-places, of ladies whose " fashionable " manners shock the propriety of German spas ; but when these scandals are the popular table-talk, in the name of justice let the woman be considered. The lord and the lady, the baronet and his wife, the parents of children, do they stand in the eyes of the world upon a level ? We hear of a man who has been compelled to part with the mother of his children, and we know that while she goes into retirement with her happiness blasted in her declining years, his car of triumph rolls on, he is still the ornament and delight of society. But when the forsaken woman glides into the shadow of suspicion, who cares to remind us that a cluster of children call her mother ; that twenty years of married life should have made her sacred ; that even her failings should have been holy to her husband ; that bitterness itself is pardonable when it rises from the fountains of love, that what by the triumphing " Lord of the Creation " is termed " incompatibility " may be nothing more than the satiety of a selfish affection ? If manliness, if chivalry, if the noble principles of honour dominate more supremely than they do in the circles of our English life, would these published separations so continually feed the mass of scandal to the detriment of names once invoked in confidence and affection at the altar ? Let cynicism utter what it will, let irony do its worst, let men affect to despise the heart-born passions, the chief happiness of every human being is at home ; neither Church nor State, nor military glory, nor political conflict, can destroy the supremacy of that instinct which makes joy itself a virtue—the pride of an honest man in his family. How implacable then must the antipathy be that breaks these consecrated bonds ; how utterly exhausted and callous must be the affection that permits this last repudiation of a moral tie, linking children with children, and teaching those children to reverence their parents.

———

As may be imagined the most desperate efforts were at this time made by FORSTER, DICKENS, and others of the " Press-gang," to stifle enquiry, or discussion on this Case. The *Times* remained silent as to all ; but its impression for July 14th, 1858, contains the following :—" LADY BULWER LYTTON.—We are requested to state, upon the best authority, that all matters in reference to this Lady, about whom certain statements have appeared in some of the public journals, are in process of being amicably settled by family arrangements, to the satisfaction of all parties concerned."

SKETCH OF LORD LYTTON.

A friend of ours, who met Lord LYTTON at dinner, favours us with an extract from his Diary, June 25, 1864, in which there is a lifelike sketch. We think it well to preserve it here. " Dined to-night with the Chief Justice, Lord HOUGHTON, and Sir BULWER LYTTON, and other senators and ladies. B. L. is the most perfect of snobs. He was shabbily dressed and sidled into the room with a slimy, slouching air and gait, and held his hat in his hand, as if he were about to drop it on the floor, and looked as if he did not know what to do with his legs, and gaped with lack-lustre eye, and said nothing, but seemed bewildered like an idiot in fine company, so that it is almost impossible to believe that he ever wrote the works which pass under his name, or, that if he did, his brain is now softening, and that he is only the wretched shadow of a man. He has a great nose like FITZBALL or BARDOLPH, only that it is not so red as the latter's; his skin is coarse and dirty; he has cut off his great beard and the hairs now look scanty and scrubby down his long, lank, lantern, Don Quixote jaws; his hair is wild and like tow ; his voice is harsh and slimy, and slobbering; he presents an appearance foul and horrid, like that of JAMES I. when hanging on that odious 'STEENIE,' and kissing his painted cheeks with swollen licking tongue. I do not know that I ever saw so odious a wretch, and I would not sit near or talk to him for a thousand pounds, poor as I am. I cannot describe his putrid corpse-like loathsomeness; I expected a fine gentleman, perhaps a fop, like his own DEVEREUX, or like BOLINGBROKE, and I saw a dirty, stupid, fish-eyed crapulous catamite—if ever human creature bore the impress of that fearful monomania. He took a lady (Mrs. R.) down to dinner, but he never spoke a word to her during the whole entertainment; he remained silent or jabbering to himself like an old orang-outang for more than an hour ; and then when he had drank more champagne than he should, he spoke the most utter rot about Denmark that ever oozed out of Avernus itself. I think COCKBURN was ashamed of him, and although he asked me specially to meet him, he did not venture to solicit my opinion of this dirty creature; but I told him mine, and related the anecdote of SAM WARREN, whom, PEARSON having one day beaten in a long legal argument before the Chief Baron, he in the exuberance of his joy bawled out to Serjeant MURPHY, 'There's a b——man of genius for you.' I told this to the C.J., and made him laugh—but he was ashamed of his dirty guest, as he could hardly fail to be. And this is the nasty animal that Lady BLESSINGTON

and her set used to call 'SHAKESPERE.'—GOD help us—I don't
wonder his wife loathed him. I am so sensitive that I believe if
he touched me with his cold gorilla paw, I should feel a pang
through my heart almost like that of Death itself. He got at
last so maudlin that he felt he could not go upstairs, and he took
his leave of the C.J. at the foot of them."

Daily Telegraph, July 15th, 1858.

In the daily business of life it is difficult and painful to sever
long-contracted bonds ; even partners in commerce bear and
forbear beyond the ordinary rules of patience, rather than break
from old connections, but how immeasurably more binding is the
compact between man and wife, how bitter is the gracelessness of
the one who rends that sacred tie, and issuing from the cloud to
the enjoyment of all the world has to give, dismisses the other
to sneers, misrepresentations, and ignominy. Not but that in
the instances present to public memory the blame of this bitter
rancour may have been divided. It is but too true that domestic
errors are wantonly magnified into crimes, that feminine sym-
pathies appeal sometimes to an unnatural code, but what is the
position of a woman in a civilised country compared with that
of a man? What is the wife when appealing against the husband? It may be that at an earlier period, as in Lady LYTTON'S
case, she has been his benefactor, his patron, and that through
long years she has been more to him than he to her ; but all
this is forgotten when the opportunity for legal separation
arrives, when children are to be parted by an attorney's document from their mother ; when malicious friends are to condole
with the injured husband, or when obtrusive advisers, who have
been unfortunate themselves, rejoice to drag down to their own
level the individual who has previously galled them by the
superiority of his personal reputation. In almost every instance
the woman is the sacrifice ; to her the public insinuations point ;
upon her contemptuous pity is lavished ; her name is set up as
a mark for jibes and insults ; she bears the miserable burden,
and her husband continues to shine as the accomplished writer,
the favoured magistrate, or the statesman expecting a peerage.

It may be beating the air to dwell on this anomaly of our
social code. While selfishness is supreme, while masculine
strength prevails over helpless right, while, in fact, the sins of
men are popularly condoned, and the mortal distempers of
women ranked as mortal sins, the scandal of a separation will
always attach to a wife as a perpetual and malignant curse, re-
echoed by every class of society ; but it may seem an object of
justice to suggest that while scandals of twenty years' duration
have been revived, while honour is recalling a thousand anec-

dotes of domestic differences and compromises, it has not been
by men that the most unpardonable injuries have been suffered.
This we say without any direct reference to the case of Lady
LYTTON. Against her, as far as we know, a calumny has never
been hinted, in spite of her ill-conceived diatribes against her
husband; but the tendency of public opinion, we are sorry to
acknowledge, runs in the direction of malevolence when the
characters of separated wives are in question. It will argue a
marked development of the national morality when, while
these transactions are under notice, some consideration is bestowed upon the possibility that when a woman has been ex-
pelled from her husband, cut off from her family interests,
buried in a social tomb, and stigmatised by her husband's repudiation, the real wrong may have been endured by herself, and
the cruelty practised by another.

After this came the letter of Mr. ROBERT LYTTON, our present
Viceroy in India, which we publish; and which speaks for itself,
even if his mother did not. How Mr. EDWIN JAMES came into
the transaction we are not told ; but the value of Mr. FORBES
WINSLOW'S certificate is well known in the profession. No one
explains how it was that this lady, who was locked up as being
insane, early in July, all of a sudden, recovered the perfect use
of her senses. Dr. CONNOLLY has got a splendid and lucrative
place since he wrote his strange certificate, and we congratulate
him upon it.

To the Editor of the " Daily Telegraph."

SIR,—As the son of Lady BULWER LYTTON, with the best
right to speak on her behalf, and so obviously with the best
means of information as to warrant the hope that my simple
assertion will be at once believed in the matter to which I am
compelled to refer, I beg to say that the statements which have
appeared in some of the public journals are exaggerated and
distorted, and that they are calculated to convey to the public
mind impressions the most erroneous and unjust. As was
natural, I put myself into constant communication with my
mother, and with the gentleman in whose family, in his private
house, she was placed (for I beg distinctly to state she was never
for a moment taken to a lunatic asylum), and I carried out the
injunctions of my father, who confided to me implicitly every
arrangement which my affection could suggest, and enjoined me
to avail myself of the advice of Lord SHAFTESBURY in whatever
was judged best and kindest for Lady LYTTON.

My mother is now with me, free from all restraint, and about,
at her own wish, to travel for a short time, in company with
myself and a female friend and relation, of her own selection.

From the moment my father felt compelled to authoıise those steps which have been made the subject of so much misrepresentation, the anxiety was to obtain the most experienced and able physician, in order that my mother should not be subject to restraint for one moment longer than was strictly justifiable. Such was his charge to me.

The certificates given by Dr. FORBES WINSLOW and Dr. CONNOLLY are subjoined, and I ought to add that Dr. CONNOLLY was the physician whom my father had requested to see Lady LYTTON; that Dr. FORBES WINSLOW was consulted by my mother's legal advisers, and I felt anxious to obtain the additional authority of the opinion of the latter gentleman, and requested my friend, Mr. EDWIN JAMES, to place himself in communication with him. I trust that such journals as have given publicity to partial and inaccurate statements will do me the justice to publish this communication, to which I need add no more than to say that this painful matter has been arranged, as it ought to be, by the members of the family whom it exclusively regards.— I have the honour to be, sir, your most obedient servant,

ROBERT B. LYTTON.

1, Park Lane, July 17th, 1858.

[Copy No. 1.]
To EDWIN JAMES, Esq., Q.C.

Having at your request examined Lady B. LYTTON this day as to her state of mind, I beg to report to you that in my opinion it is such as to justify her liberation from restraint.

I think it but an act of justice to Sir EDWARD B. LYTTON to state that upon the facts which I have ascertained were submitted to him, and upon the certificates of the medical men * whom he was advised to consult, the course which he has pursued throughout these painful proceedings cannot be considered harsh or unjustifiable.—I remain, sir, your obedient servant,

FORBES WINSLOW, M.D., D.C.L.

23, Cavendish square, July 16th, 1858.

[Copy No. 2.]

London, July 17th, 1858.

SIR,—Notwithstanding the decided opinion which I felt it my duty to express with reference to Lady LYTTON, after my visit

---

* The " medical men " here referred to are Mr. ROSS, an apothecary, of Farringdon street, City, and Mr. HALE THOMPSON, of Clarges-street, formerly connected with the Westminster Hospital.

to her at the private residence of Mr. and Mrs. HILL, and which
I need not repeat, justified the course you adopted; I have
much satisfaction in hearing of the arrangements which have
been made for her ladyship leaving their family in the society of
her son and her female friend.—I have the honour to be, sir,
very faithfully, your obedient servant,

G. CONNOLLY, M.D.

To the Right Hon. Sir EDW. BULWER LYTTON,
    Bart., M.P., &c., &c., &c.

The whole of this is, no doubt, full of satisfaction to all persons concerned; and to the outside world. We own that it does
not satisfy us: but then perhaps *we* belong to the discontented.
Our readers have only to bear in mind that at this time Sir
E. B. L. was a Cabinet Minister, with all the immense resources
of that post; that he was backed up by the QUEEN, by Lord
DERBY, and Mr. DISRAELI; and that under such circumstances
any attempt to "make the worse appear the better cause" could
have little doubt of perfect success. Such appears to have
been the opinion of the writer of what follows :—

To the Editor of the " Daily Telegraph."

SIR,—Thanks to you for your noble and eloquent defence of
Lady LYTTON, and the outrage on public justice perpetrated by
her husband. Your watchfulness may have been rendered
unnecessary by the family "arrangement" which has been
announced, but heaven help Lady LYTTON travelling abroad under
the guardianship of such "affection," with the stigma of insanity
upon her, available for any purpose.

The letter of Mr. ROBERT LYTTON explains nothing, answers
nothing. It does not even show where his mother is. He writes
—"My mother is now with me, free from all restraint." This
letter is dated 1, Park-lane, the town residence of Sir BULWER
LYTTON, who is now in London. Does Mr. LYTTON mean to say
that his mother is or was on Saturday last under the roof of her
husband? There is more than meets the eye in this. Is Lady
LYTTON free from all restraint? Whatever the "arrangement"
is, it was made when she was in durance, and not a free agent,
and if that arrangement has taken her from the custody of
Mr. HILL, of Brentford, to that of her own son and husband, it
is only that her prison-house has been changed. "From the
moment my father felt compelled to authorise those steps which
have been made the subject of so much misrepresentation, &c.,
in order that my mother should not be subject to restraint for
one moment longer than was strictly justifiable, such was his
charge to me." If Sir EDWARD was so solicitous to procure the
opinions of the most able physicians, we may ask how it
happened that instead of consulting Dr. FORBES WINSLOW and

Dr. CONNOLLY in the first instance, that he employed a Mr. THOMPSON to kidnap the lady at his own residence. Mr. LYTTON says the statements are "exaggerated" and "distorted," but he does not explain how. He says he has the best right to speak on behalf of his mother, and has "the best means of information," and that his assertion will be at once believed. It is hard to refuse this to a son, and in ordinary cases one would not feel inclined to do so; but he seems to have acted entirely under the influence of the father, and to have been from first to last so directly opposed to his mother, that before we give him the credence he asks there are several questions he ought to answer. Is it true he has neither sought after nor corresponded with his mother, nor even seen her, for nearly seventeen years, until he met her at the Hustings, at Hertford, during the recent election there? Is it true that on that occasion he made the preliminary attempt which culminated at the house of Mr. THOMPSON, in Clarges-street, to put his mother in a madhouse by sending a physician to the house of the Mayor of Hertford where she was on a visit? Is it true that when his mother was kidnapped in Clarges-street, and Miss RYVES ran out into the street, and seeing Mr. LYTTON waiting outside, entreated him to interfere and procure assistance to prevent his mother being carried off to Brentford, he refused to have anything to do with the matter? Other questions suggest themselves, not directly affecting Mr. LYTTON, but important to an understanding of this painful case. He says, "I put myself in constant communication with my mother. . . . I carried out the injunctions of my father, who confided in me implicitly, . . . enjoined me to avail myself of the advice of Lord SHAFTESBURY in whatever was judged best and kindest for Lady LYTTON." Is this a solemn farce, a piece of well-acted hypocrisy, or a truth in letter and spirit? Is it conceivable that Sir EDWARD LYTTON, not having set eyes on his wife for seventeen years, and leaving her to live and suffer and complain during all that time on £400 a year, suddenly became tenderly solicitous on her behalf, as to require "all that was best and kindest" should be done for her? Why is Lord SHAFTESBURY introduced? Is it to give the shelter of his sanctity to a cruel outrage? MEPHISTOPHELES might envy the genius which suggested the mention of Lord SHAFTESBURY as the adviser and referee of Sir BULWER LYTTON.

The certificates appended to Mr. LYTTON's letter are not properly "certificates;" they are intended as apologies for the conduct of Sir BULWER LYTTON. But though put forward with this view, they substantiate that the state of Lady LYTTON's mind "is such as to justify her liberation from restraint," and prove nothing to his honour. It is easy to see that the "certificate" of Dr. FORBES WINSLOW is but an answer to certain questions put by Mr. EDWIN JAMES, who was strangely employed by Mr. LYTTON, and whose object was to extract from the doctor everything that he could on behalf of Sir EDWARD. On this part of the question we are all competent to form an opinion, and if it should appear that the facts submitted to Sir EDWARD were facts suggested by himself, and the medical men, on whose certificates he acted, were employed by him, which is the fact, Dr. FORBES WINSLOW's opinion upon this part of the question goes for nothing.

The more enquiries we make into the matter the more convinced we are that a great wrong was attempted, and has now been glossed over. That wrong was not done to Lady LYTTON alone, but to all society. Her wrath may have been appeased, her personal wounds may have received a plaister, and her friends may have been flattered and cajoled into silence, but is the public satisfied, or the wrong to society been atoned for, while the case of Lady LYTTON remains uninvestigated, and the conduct of her husband escapes official and public censure? Is any one of us safe so long as the law permits the "next of kin" to do what has been done to her?

AN ENGLISHMAN.

Daily Telegraph, July 21, 1858.

We return unwillingly, and, we trust, for the last time, to the melancholy scandal in which Sir BULWER LYTTON has involved himself. It had been our intention not to carry further this painful controversy, yet additional explanations are extorted from us by the peculiar tactics not only of particular individuals, but of some among our contemporaries. There have been allusions to "misrepresentations" contained in "paragraphs," and "exaggerated and distorted statements," circulated with reference to the Lady, who a few days since was spirited away by stratagem to Brentford. Now in respect of the persons principally concerned, nothing more need be said; if the Right Hon. Secretary for the Colonies has effected a settlement agreeable to his conscience and his wife, none has a right to interfere; if the Electors of Hertford are satisfied, the general public has perhaps little reason to complain, and if legality and justice are not to be permanently outraged we rejoice that family negociations have been successful. Yet there are points connected with our own position, which should be clearly set forth. The vague and solemn rebukes that have been set forth were addressed almost exclusively to ourselves, not of paragraphs, but of articles based upon a well-prepared narrative published in a provincial journal, no one assertion of which to the present moment has been invalidated. But if there has been " exaggeration," if there has been " falsity," who was the person and what was the time to correct them ? The proper individual was the son of Sir BULWER LYTTON himself, and the proper time was upon one of the occasions, when since the exposure in our columns, he called at the *Daily Telegraph* office, sometimes not alone. Did we hear then anything about " distortion " or " misrepresentation " ? Most certainly not a word. Mr. ROBERT LYTTON acted then as the champion of his mother, and not he only, but her personal friends also appeared delighted that upon public grounds an appeal had been made, bearing so directly upon their private interests. Then, we think, was the moment for substituting accurate for erroneous impressions; but since this retort is forced upon us, what if we suggest if the original case was not one to be explained away ? Lady LYTTON was by no means the person interested in a concealment of the facts or in hushing up the affair before it was dragged before a Commission of Lunacy. We are now told, indeed, that the Baronet was satisfied in the course he adopted, which we have never pretended to deny, for we have insisted only on enquiry. We asked whether the allegations against him were true, and we pointed out the impossibility of allowing a public man to remain under an imputation so scathing, and we expressed our hope that the sinister rumours afloat would be set at rest by an ample vindication of the Privy Councillor's conduct. Is it our fault then that no such vindication has been attempted—that Sir BULWER LYTTON has preferred a private arrangement—that he has defied the written opinion of two professional men, and allowed his so-called insane Wife to be once more at large upon terms to which he had previously refused his consent? Nothing would have been more satisfactory to ourselves and the public than that Lord DERBY's Colonial Secretary, after a strict judicial investigation, should have demonstrated himself a Man of Honour, incapable of kidnapping an obnoxious Wife.

But upon whose authority was Lady LYTTON captured and sent to Brentford ? Not originally, as has been stated, upon that of Dr. CONNOLLY. The certificates were signed by a Mr. HALE THOMPSON, once known at Westminster Hospital, and by a Mr. ROSS, an apothecary of Farringdon-street, whose medical reputation seems to have travelled providentially from east of Temple-bar to an official residence in Downing-street. The sanction of these " eminent " gentlemen enabled the policemen and nurses to place Lady LYTTON by force in a carriage, but through a humane after-thought, Dr. CONNOLLY was ultimately called in and dispatched to the residence of Mr. ROBERT GARDINER HILL, at Brentford. There he certified that Lady LYTTON was a demented patient; there, however, Dr. FORBES WINSLOW, within a day or two, certified in singularly cautious and ambiguous terms, that she was *not* a demented patient; she was in fact fit and unfit to live without restraint, and the result is that with her son and a female relation, she is to enjoy a continental tour. At all events, it is gratifying to know that whatever has been the effect on the Lady's nerves, she has been benefitted by the public discussion of her case. Instead of the Brentford process, she will sojourn at the Spas, and Florentine gaiety may compensate her for a week of Middlesex gloom under the Lunacy Law.

Concerning the Brentford question, Mr. ROBERT GARDINER HILL is pleased to think himself aggrieved. We may remark that Mr. HILL claims to have penetrated the secrets of physiological science. That he is not the proprietor of a " notorious Madhouse " we will admit, if he will allow that he is the principal of a " celebrated Lunatic Asylum."

What consolation would it be to any of our readers, if falsely accused of insanity, that a " lunatic asylum," and not a " madhouse," shuts its doors upon them. Would a paltry verbal quibble reconcile them to captivity among maniacs and the mentally afflicted? He is among the proprietors, he confesses, of Wyke House, which, if he will not permit us to describe it as "notorious," is at least well-known as a Madhouse, or, if the term be offensive, of a Lunatic Asylum.

Though not standing alone in this controversy, we have been solitary among the organs of the press in claiming a public enquiry on behalf of Lady LYTTON. In our main object we have succeeded. The " patient " is no longer in legal or in medical clutches. Her position has totally changed since the protest of public indignation rose against the treatment to which she had been subject. The Taunton people are satisfied that a great wrong is not to be perpetrated, and Lady LYTTON's friends, who rejoiced in the original exposure, are now at liberty to be as ungrateful as they please. They will not induce us, at all events, to state whence our information was derived, or how far the Right Honourable Baronet is indebted to themselves for the publication of a monstrous scandal. But it was due to ourselves, to our readers, and to the innumerable correspondents whose letters we have felt it necessary to suppress, to remind Mr. ROBERT LYTTON and his colleagues in the negociation just concluded, that they have to thank the press for the publicity which spared them the painful alternative of a judicial investigation. It fell to us, fortunately, to produce a movement of public opinion in favour of Lady LYTTON ; and it is not for her personal advocates to blame the persistency with which we have followed it to its final issue. Least of all, whatever gracelessness may be exhibited in Park-lane, do we regret a course of proceedings without which, in all probability, the wife of Sir BULWER LYTTON might have been still, and possibly for the rest of her life, subject to the galling tendernesses of our Asylums for Lunatics.

LORD LYTTON THE FIRST.

This man was once called by his admirers (who were probably well paid for it) " The modern SHAKSPERE." We now know in what estimation his writings are held. But his private character was so vile and detestable, that it will cause almost incredulity if it ever should be exposed in its true colours to the world. Mr. LABOUCHERE, in *Truth*, has a paragraph upon him, which is truth itself. Here it is :—"A man may be endowed with genius and with numerous amiable qualities, and yet be a Snob. Few of those who have lived during the present century have been gifted with more genius than Lord LYTTON, and yet few have been so arrant a Snob. In his works of fiction he has frequently sought to portray gentlemen, and these gentlemen, each of whom has a family likeness to his creator, are the beau-ideals of Snobs—clever, pushing, conceited, florid Snobs, with Brummagem manners, Brummagem morals, a Brummagem varnish of philosophy, and a Brummagem varnish of poetry." In Friday's *Times* we read this advertisement, anything meaner than which we never perused :—

HERTS, Knebworth-park, with 1,500 acres of capital Shooting, three miles from Stevenage and Welwyn Stations (G.N.R.)—A handsome FURNISHED baronial MANSION, surrounded by a fine park and splendid gardens and grounds. Particulars of &c., &c.

Is the son as mean a fellow as the father ? Lord LYTTON left him about £300,000 ; and he is paid as Viceroy of India £100,000 a year, with "pickings;" and he offers to let his family mansion. Would he not do better to let his Mother, that noble, injured Lady, into Knebworth, than hire it out to some stranger?

MR. JOHN FORSTER.

This man, who was one of Lord LYTTON's tools, and who also played toady for the greater part of his life to a congenial evil spirit, Sir ALEXANDER COCKBURN, is thus described by Lady LYTTON. Under the name of JANUS ALLPUFF, she alludes to her accomplished husband :—"The chief MECÆNAS of this FUDGESTER (FORSTER) is a Sir JANUS ALLPUFF, who not content with having hunted his unhappy Wife nearly to death, and reduced to the lowest ebb of pecuniary destitution, from defending herself against his infamous Conspiracies, also prevents her in every possible way from earning her bread : and who so useful in this way as FUDGESTER? I should tell you, in order to show you the astuteness and diabolical cunning of this Infamous Gang, and the tortuous sneaking measures they adopt to prevent their dirty work being brought home to them, by always employing others, as far a-field as possible, to do it ; this FUDGESTER, from being a known tool and toady of that vile old profligate, Sir JANUS ALLPUFF, and a declared enemy of his Victim, never reviews her books, or mentions her name in any way, in his own particular paper, *The Excruciator (The Examiner)*, but merely sets on the ramifications of the Gang to attack and malign her in every possible way : and from the wording of some of these attacks, it is quite clear that Sir JANUS gives the substance of what he wishes them to do, as the same internal evidence exists of such being the case, that does as to his furnishing the pith of the puffs about himself to those organs of his myrmidons. But after all there is nothing so silly as your over-cunning people ; which the very bungling way in which Sir JANUS gets his dirty work done, will ultimately prove : and indeed some of the anonymous letters which his infamous Literary Myrmidons are set to write to his Victim, strongly resemble, in their little mean cramped characters, his own, or his JACKAL FUDGESTER'S writing."

THE LATE DUKE OF ATHOL.

One of VICTORIA'S chief favourites, and one who knew a little more of her than we think it well to publish, was one of the BULWER LYTTON Gang, and is thus described :—

Another member of this worshipful clique of Stop-at-nothings, a few grades higher as to station, but quite on a par as to blackguardism, is the Duke of TWILGLENON.

"Ah, I've seen that horrid fellow," broke in Mr. PHIPPEN ; "what a horrid-looking Wretch it is—for all the world like a low, drunken Grazier in appearance, looking as if he had just beaten or worried one of the poor animals he had been driving, to death."

" Well, sir, I believe he does kick and worry the only animal which every Englishman has a right to ill-treat to any amount, which is his wife ; for beautiful and amiable as the poor Duchess is, it don't prevent her being well brutalized by her ruffianly-looking husband. ● Ah, sir, I often think that had Princess CHARLOTTE lived, *she* would have had some feeling for her own sex, and that such notoriously profligate men as this Duke of TWILGLENON, and his worthy associate, that Sir JANUS ALLPUFF, would not have disgraced the English Court. But perhaps a man in my sphere of life is no judge of such matters; only I cannot help thinking, according to the Laws of GOD, Vice is Vice, and Infamy is Infamy, all over the world, whether in Queens, or Dukes, or Dustmen, or in Baronets or Bricklayers."

"To be sure it is," said Mr. PHIPPEN, "only ten times worse in the Patrician than in the Plebeian, as *they* have not even the excuses of misery, as provocation, to drive them into low vice."

But Sir JANUS ALLPUFF had other irons in the fire.

I am not aware, even from the insight I have had into the Sodom and Gomorrah of the literary world, that it is customary for Reviewers (?) previous to reviewing a work, to write *anonymous* letters to the author, stating that theirs was rather an influential Review, but that before they reviewed her last work, they must first assure her that the world did not care one straw whether she was well-used or ill-used, but *they* (the *Reviewer*, mind, and the Writer of the *anonymous* letters, for there were two) wished to know was it possible that she meant Mr.——, one of the characters in the novel, for her own husband?—as though they should ask, "Is it possible you have dared to blaspheme your GOD!!" though indeed, among *that* class of notoriously infamous and profligate men, who have left *no* law of GOD unviolated, Husbands of course are generally given precedence to the Almighty in the awe and reverence such men endeavour to inculcate in the female slaves of Great Britain. Now, with regard to that, the authoress had only to say "that it was impossible to write a novel without having bad characters in it, and it would be equally impossible to mention *any* vice or any meanness which would not be perfectly applicable, and which therefore might not appear *personal* to Sir JANUS ALLPUFF, who having taken high degrees in them *all*, was at perfect liberty to take his choice, and fit them on as he pleased; and as for the sacredness of the mere word *husband*, as to *her* it was only the synonyme of the most extreme personal violence and brutality, terminating in being turned out of her home to make way for her legal tyrant's mistresses, and to having had one child destroyed physically and the other morally, being swindled out of every shilling, and hunted by a relentless Fiend through the world, it could not be very sacred, *quoique sacré*, to her." "Oh, but respect to her position," said Conventionality; *he* had not left *her any* save one of honest superiority, which, as it arose from herself, it was not in *his* nor in his myrmidon's power to deprive her of. Then what *was* she to respect? Surely *not* the iniquitous laws that allowed a woman to be so treated, nor the vicious and immoral society which tolerates such conduct; and least of all the opinion of a certain obsequious clique of the press, which panders to, puffs, and protects such infamy. The silliest thing that ever tyrant did is to leave his slave *nothing* to lose, to hope, or to fear, for *then* comes the reaction: the pigmy springs into an armed giant, and the trampled worm is, *for the sake of others*, willing to become a martyr to a cause of which they have been so long a Victim; and of this overreaching folly the clever Sir JANUS ALLPUFF had been guilty. "Oh! but his talents," simpers some Miss, to whom they no doubt appear, as compared with her own, *very great;* but his Victim, being an exceedingly well-read Woman, could not even bow down to and worship *them*, looking upon him much in the light of the ass which carried the relics, from having read the most of his works *in the authors from whom he transferred them;* and, moreover, having more original ideas in her own head than *he* ever purloined from anybody else's. So, finding there was nothing to be done with a Wretch of this kind, and that he could not even hunt her to death, it was necessary to make the Clique set up a hue-and-cry about the *personality* of her books; but *who* more personal, pray, without the excuse of gross outrage that *she* had had, than Sir JANUS himself, even to formerly ridiculing the *Assinæum* and others of his now obedient vassals, to say nothing of his converting Her Majesty's ministry into highwaymen? Who more personal, either, than his friend Mr. JERICHO JABBER, in his Caucasian romances? And who *so* personal, without any regard to *vraisemblance*, much less to *truth*, as my Lady GORGON, * in her trashy productions? But because *she* has made her house *convenient* to the English aristocracy for the last quarter of a century, she has a pension of three hundred a-year, while poor HAYDON starved on an under-footman's wages of twenty-five—Shame! Shame! But Sir JANUS had not done with his victim yet. *The New Quarterly, The Literary Gazette,* in old SILENUS JERDAN'S most unscrupulous strain, so that his reminiscences seemed to hiccup through every line; *The Assinæum*, and, in short, *all* Sir JANUS' *special tools* and literary bravoes—

"Cursed by the goose's and the critic's quill,"

were ordered to affect to treat her book as the production of a mad woman. Nay, more, BOB CLAPPER, † another star of this galaxy, and *quite worthy of being one*, considering that he lives with another man's wife and is always drunk, was also set to *bell* all over London that Sir JANUS's victim was mad, which really was very unfair towards FUDGESTER, as they had just concocted a job appointment for him, and inducted him into it, under the very appropriate title of Purveyor of Lunatics to the Literary Fund. But if Sir JANUS had only had the goodness, instead of *saying* and telling his gang to say all this, *to have instituted a medical inquiry, or any other inquiry*, that could have

---

* Lady MORGAN.

† BOB CLAPPER—the late Mr. ROBERT BELL, author of "Marriage, a Comedy." JERICHO JABBER is DISRAELI.

his Wife's conduct and his own *examined into, thoroughly sifted, and brought before the public,* she would have been, and still would be, infinitely obliged to him.　But no! the calumnies of this most loathsome and utterly contemptible *Clique,* like their *charities* (?), are upon the principle of *publicity* and *self-security.* With regard to the former, they stab in the back and in the dark ; with regard to the latter—*via* the *Times*—they dip their hands into other people's pockets ; and no matter, as far as Sir JANUS ALLPUFF is concerned, if his Victim wife has been hunted down to the lowest straits of pecuniary destitution, as long as *his* name figures in £100 subscriptions for restoring Churches, or any other sound-of-trumpet doings, he will still have the Reverend Incumbent of any living in *his* gift, swearing that he is a reformed character!! and FUDGESTER endeavouring to demonstrate to the British public, by dint of brass and ink, that what *might* have the appearance of a bare-faced plagiary in others, is the highest proof and evidence of profound *originality* in Sir JANUS ALLPUFF, and that *so* any *generous* critic must admit ; and certainly it is very easy for critics, *à la* FUDGESTER, to be generous with other people's property, and there is no generosity in giving people what they don't want ; so FUDGESTER is quite right to give *his* friends as much honour, originality, and generosity as he possibly can.　But it was not to be supposed that the clever Sir JANUS, with such a *corps d'esprit* (?) at his command, would let his Victim rest ; so he next sets a fellow calling himself a theatrical manager (?), of the name of " LEYTON," to write to her, demanding permission to dramatise one of her Novels.　Now the motive of this was two-fold : first, it inculpated the rare jest of leading the poor, struggling, financially-crippled Wife to suppose that she was about to get a little money, which would be a great godsend to her, considering the terrible embarrassments his ceaseless conspiracies had entailed on her ; and next, it established a correspondence under the pretext of arranging the scenes and condensing the plot of the play, which correspondence was drawled out over the space of several months, which of course kept Sir JANUS perfectly in possession of his Victim's whereabouts.　But at length even such a very bungling plotter as this very *"clever"* man felt the hum of the play could not last for ever ; consequently the plot began to thicken, and the *soi-disant* Mr. LEYTON was sent with a woman, who had every appearance of being a street-walker, in *person,* and under the name of BARNES.　This phase of the plot consisted in getting into the same house as Sir JANUS's victim, and giving her the trouble and expense of getting out of it ; and at a later period of the plot, this low fellow BARNES wrote her a most infamous letter, the handwriting of which was precisely the same as the letters of the *soi-disant* LEYTON.　But as Sir JANUS ALLPUFF

invariably adopts the opposite *verbal* virtue to the particular vice
he may be at the moment practising, about this time he was
seized in the House of Commons with such a *"generous"* (a
favourite *word* of his) horror of the under-hand and the anonymous, that *he* would like to have every article in a newspaper
signed with the writer's name! But surely he must have uttered
this *fanfarronade* under the full conviction that such an absurd
law never would or could be passed; for otherwise, what dreadful high wages some of his doers of dirty work would require
for some of the paragraphs, *pro* and *con.*, which they are ordered
to indite! Shocking to think of! for it almost makes one see, in
one's mind's eye, Sir JANUS *himself* reduced to such a state of
pecuniary destitution as not to have coin sufficient to pay for a
raspberry puff, much less for a literary one! Thus hunted out
of the miserable and remote village in which she had taken
refuge, Sir JANUS's victim left it, not letting anyone know the
place she was going to, which so exasperated her tyrant to think
that she should for even a week, a day, or an hour, escape from
his persecutions, that the next time the miserable pittance he
doles out to her became due, and from which he even deducts
the Income Tax! he positively refused to pay it to one of her
solicitors till he had a clergyman's certificate from the place
where she then was, *guaranteeing that she was alive*, and this he no
doubt thought a very *clever* way of finding out where she was. But
honesty is always not only braver, but shrewder, than rascality, not
only because it has nothing to fear, but because all resources are
within its grasp, and as his Victim was determined not to yield to
this disgusting, though too ridiculous, piece of petty tyranny—a
very clever lawyer of hers, and one as honest as he is clever, soon
brought that contemptible wretch Sir JANUS and his rascally
attorney to his senses by writing them word what he would do if
this disgraceful swindle which he calls an allowance was not paid
instantly. Of course he soon hunted out his Victim again, but
his spy (everyone being now forewarned) was sent about her
business in a manner that must have rather surprised her and
her "gifted" employer, and as now there is a talk of a general
election, with what he himself and FUDGESTER would call those
"high and generous instincts" for his own safety which never
quit him, I suppose he will keep quiet for some little time, and
he had better!

"What a contemptible, dastardly set of Blackguards, to be
sure!"

"You'd say so, sir, if you knew as much of them as I do."

"Egad! I think you've told me quite enough. How old is
this Sir JANUS ALLPUFF, and what sort of a looking fellow
is he?"

"Well, sir, in years, I don't believe he is much more than

fifty, but from the horrible life he has led he looks eighty ; however, in the puffs, of course, all this is attributed to his literary labours.   His person is not so easy to describe ; it is the head of a goat on the body of a grasshopper.   But it's the expression of his face that is so horrible ; the lines in it make it look like an intersected map of Vice, bounded on one side by the Black Sea of Hypocrisy, on the other by the Falsehood Mountains."

INDEX TO "A BLIGHTED LIFE."

INDEX TO SUPPLEMENTAL NOTES.

THE END.